RUNNING
THROUGH
THE WALL

RUNNING THROUGH THE WALL

A Guide for the Serious Runner

by Raymond Bridge

THE DIAL PRESS · *New York* ·

Published by
The Dial Press
1 Dag Hammarskjold Plaza
New York, New York 10017

Manufactured in the United States of America

FIRST PRINTING

Design by Dennis J. Grastorf

LIBRARY OF CONGRESS CATALOGING IN PUBLICATION DATA

Bridge, Raymond.
  Running through the wall.

  Bibliography: p. 213
  1. Running—Training. I. Title.
GV1061.5.B74   796.4'26   80-10838
ISBN 0-8037-7609-8

To Maddie,
who, better than anyone else I have ever met,
knows the art of balancing life's pleasures
with its responsibilities

CONTENTS

ficiency and aerobic working level. Body weight. Joints, tendons, and skeletal structure. Summary.

INTRODUCTION

TRANSCENDING BARRIERS AND overcoming obstacles are characteristic activities of runners at every level, from the overweight office worker trying to reverse the effects of twenty-five years of sedentary existence to the Olympic contender exploring the limits of human physical performance. Some of these obstacles are physical ones and some are psychological. Often it is difficult to separate the limitations of the body from those of the mind even after a hurdle has been jumped. The metaphor of the barrier, hurdle, or wall seems appropriate to running, however, because progress so often comes by fits and starts. The runner reaches a plateau, and it seems for a while that no amount of effort will bring any progress beyond it. Then suddenly everything falls together and advances are made daily. For many runners these doldrums and spurts of progress occur without rhyme or reason, in a cycle that seems almost perversely fortuitous. In fact, the results of our training are usually quite predictable, but the rhythm of training follows a different pattern than the one expected by many runners. As a result of this misunderstanding the barriers are often more familiar than the satisfying periods of progress.

The wall in the title of this book is not only the famed wall encountered by so many runners around the twenty-mile mark of the marathon. Progress in running involves breaking through a whole series of barriers, which fade to insignificance once we have passed beyond them, but which often seem impossibly massive until we do. As with the marathon wall, most of these barriers are really built up or overcome in the months before they are actually encountered. It is the training miles put in long before a particular marathon that enable the runner to continue at a steady pace for twenty-six miles or to run with a particular strategy in the race, knowing that it will not backfire during the last few miles. Similarly, the runner who has trained properly peaks for the big races not by accident but through careful planning.

Training with an understanding of what you are trying to accomplish, and of the way each daily run fits into the plan, is even more important for the beginner and the runner of moderate experience than for the veteran racer. Disappointing races, injuries, failure to progress, and frustrating slumps are very common among less experienced runners who have taken up the sport seriously. Most of these disappointments are due to a lack of understanding of the roles of different training methods. As a result many runners have no coherent idea of what they are doing. They don't work out training programs that can reasonably be expected to allow them to improve at a good rate, and they fail to learn from their mistakes because of a lack of understanding of which methods have worked for them and which have not. Misguided training slows down progress, and many runners who love the sport end up unnecessarily injured or seriously discouraged.

WHAT THIS BOOK IS ABOUT

Running Through the Wall is an attempt to present a coherent explanation of training techniques for serious runners. It is designed to help you to devise your own training plans and schedules and to modify them in light of your own experience. I have tried to provide a framework of understanding within which you can mix your runs and schedules to suit your own needs with some anticipation of what sort of results you can expect. A clear conception of your training goals and techniques will also provide a means of interpreting the results afterwards, so that you can come up with a more effective program in the future. It makes no sense to go out and run a set of all-out 220-yard intervals just because you have heard that they work for a particular champion or a locally successful runner. The intervals might be an ideal regimen for you at one stage of your training and a disastrous one at another. You should have a reason for thinking that intervals of that type would work for you at a particular time. When you have seen the effects later on, you will then have increased your understanding of your body and its needs, because you will know whether the prescription worked. Mixing training techniques at random is like tossing in the ingredients of a casserole at random: You rarely achieve good results, and you don't learn to choose the elements any better on your next attempt. As with a school of cooking, a set of training principles gives you both a better chance of immediate success and a basis for improving and refining your combinations of ingredients as you go along.

In outlining a framework for developing training routines, I have not attempted to set out any kind of rigid structure, prescribing a particular series of distances to be run during a base training period or a set formula for speed work. There are a whole range of programs that will work for any runner; and while one recipe will work perfectly for some runners, different combinations will work better for others. The crucial point is to understand what you are trying to accomplish and how each training session fits into your complete program. The ideas presented in this book fall into an overall pattern; but the pattern is a flexible one, easily adjusted to suit individual needs, abilities, and available time. No training schedule can serve the individual well if it is followed slavishly. Even the most rigid training theories advocated by some coaches are designed to be modified to fit the progress of a particular athlete. With a good background in training principles, there is no reason why the runner cannot successfully work out his or her own program.

It should be clear from the various training methods followed by successful athletes that no one theory represents the last word on the subject. The ideas presented in this book have worked for quite a few people, but there is room for argument about any of them. No attempt has been made here to catalogue all the possible areas of disagreement; it should suffice to say that there are many. There are successful distance runners who try to stay at top form all the time, or at least for long periods, rather than peaking and then retreating to base training. There are good runners who never run speed work in training and others who never run anything else.

Scientific research is often cited in this book to explain certain training ideas or theories. It is important to note, however, that scientific knowledge about running performance and training methods provides a basis for argument but very few final answers. Research in many areas related to running is incomplete, and the results are contradictory. The simplified scientific data mentioned in the pages that follow are simply to provide the runner with a basis for understanding the relationships between training, racing, and the changes that take place in the body.

THE SERIOUS RUNNER

This book, unlike my earlier *Runner's Book,* is intended primarily for the serious runner rather than for the beginner or the nonrunner who is thinking of taking up the sport. The beginner may find useful information here as well, but the reader will not encounter many pages devoted to the advantages of running or much attention to typical beginners' problems. The serious runner has long since learned that he or she can run a distance of several miles, gotten past the stage of huffing and puffing after jogging for five minutes, and learned to deal with trivial problems like minor chafing and finding comfortable clothes to run in.

By "serious runner," however, I don't mean to include only those racers who are serious contenders in big races. There are many others who enjoy the sport and consider it important—often training for as many hours each week as Bill Rodgers or Frank Shorter—and yet have no delusions of grandeur or designs on world records. Their training problems vary somewhat, depending on their experience and weekly mileage; but whether they run three miles a day or fifteen, they have more in common with one another than they do with the true beginner.

Consider an example among fairly good runners. Many very strong marathoners in the top class average around 100 miles of training a week. A top marathoner might average 6½ minutes per mile in training, going considerably faster some of the time, and dropping off to 7 minutes per mile during some long, slow distance runs. Such a runner would average a little under eleven hours of running a week, not counting showers, dressing, stretching, and the like. The typical 3-hour marathoner, just good enough to qualify for the Boston Marathon, would spend just as much time on the roads running 70 miles a week at an average of 8½ minutes per mile. Clearly the two runners are quite different classes in competition. The two put just as much effort into the sport, however, drive themselves out of bed in the dark winter mornings just as often, and have to be just as careful to avoid injury. Both take their running seriously, or they would not run so much mileage month in and month out.

The 5-mile-a-day runner falls into a somewhat different category of condition and attitude about the sport, but still has far more in common with those who run marathons regularly than with a newcomer to the sport. This book is intended for regular runners with varying degrees of experience at different training levels.

RUNNING AND RACING

Active runners have widely varying attitudes toward racing. For some of them racing is the main goal of running, or at least the focal point of the rest of their running. For others racing is the antithesis of everything they enjoy about the sport. It is structured, artificial, and competitive—the characteristics that they run to escape. Probably the majority of dedicated runners in the United States fall somewhere in between these extremes. They may take the races they run seriously, but their main goal is not tied to racing success. Still other runners race occasionally because they find low-key distance racing to be fun and because it is an enjoyable excuse to get together with other runners. Many race from time to time simply to provide a specific orientation for their daily running. This sort of attitude may provide a little extra incentive to get up on a cold, rainy morning when the temptation to roll over and go back to sleep is great, or give the recreational runner a motive for doing interval training that might not otherwise exist.

There are dedicated runners all along the spectrum of attitudes toward racing, and their goals in training are likely to be somewhat different. The serious racer has to be far more concerned about peaking for particular races and is likely to do a good deal more speed work than runners who race casually or not at all. There are also quite a few runners who put in more than 100 miles a week but rarely enter a race. They are just as serious about their running as the racers, but they find different sorts of satisfaction.

This book is not oriented particularly toward racing, though for convenience the discussion often uses racing terminology. This is useful in discussing training, because it provides a shorthand reference for distance, speed, running style, and the like. In giving training recommendations, a certain amount of precision is important to avoid serious misunderstanding. There is an enormous difference between someone who runs mountain trails for a couple of hours at a relaxed pace of six minutes a mile and a person who runs for the same length of time at half that speed. Suitable training routines for the first person would result in exhaustion or a torn Achilles tendon for the second.

Thus, I hope that antiracers will forgive the racing terminology that is frequently used in this book. Marathon-style training, for example, does not have to be oriented toward a marathon. The very use of the term *training* has negative connotations for some people who have had bad experiences with endless laps around a track. But *training* does not have to mean training *for* racing; it merely implies that some thought is given during one's daily running to the long-term effects in conditioning the body. If you want to run farther, a certain pattern of running is desirable. To develop speed over a certain range of distance, still another general pattern will produce better results. Even those runners who do not time their runs or measure distances are usually interested in improving the ease and grace with which they can move over favorite courses, and we all compare our performances from day to day in some fashion.

The purpose of this book is to help you to improve your running in whatever direction is most important to you, and to help avoid unproductive dead ends and injuries along the way. Running is most enjoyable when you can avoid frustrating setbacks and debilitating injuries. It should be a joy, not a chore. May you have many happy miles on the roads and trails.

ACKNOWLEDGMENTS

Few of the ideas presented in this book are original, though the sorting out of the useful suggestions and theories from those that didn't work is largely a product of my own experience and that of many running companions with whom I have discussed problems, solutions, and training methods. It is difficult to trace the genesis of one's ideas about a subject like running; when you run every day, you develop your own ideas, sometimes independently, sometimes by drawing on others, and it is not always clear where a thought began. I am indebted to many people who have written about running and others who have shared their thoughts and experiences with me while on the run. Some of the people of whose influence I am most conscious are Ken Young, many of whose ideas I absorbed secondhand from my friend Charles Fuselier; Ron Dawes, author of *The Self-Made Olympian;* Tom Osler, author of many articles on running; and my fellow members of the Fat Men's and Sheepdogs' Early Morning Marching Society, Ron and Ollie, with whom I shared many an early morning stumble. Obviously, like every author, I am responsible for my own mistakes, misreadings, and wayward runs.

RUNNING THROUGH THE WALL

CHAPTER I

THOUGHTS ON THE RUN

THE JOYS OF running have been expounded again and again, sometimes to the point of wretched excess. As runners we sometimes don the mantles of prophets preaching the gospel of fitness to the heathen multitudes. We bore our friends, drive our spouses to distraction, and make the lives of nonrunners at parties miserable. Smokers flee our ostentatious coughing, and the overweight do their best to escape our sermons on the virtues of exercise and cardiopulmonary conditioning. Almost every dedicated runner has been guilty of these offenses at one time or another. They are sometimes hard to avoid in the flush of discovering the pleasures of being fit.

We have expounded the virtues of running so much, too, that it is easy to forget the darker side of the sport. Many runners are injured—not in the ways predicted by the doom sayers, such as heart attacks or damage to the joints and spine that carry over into everyday life, but in ways that nonetheless are extremely serious for the person to whom running has become an important part of life. The injuries strike hardest not at the casual jogger, but rather at the serious runner who takes up the sport with great enthusiasm, begins preparing for or running marathons, and pushes middle-aged joints beyond their capacity to adapt. Runners' circles are filled with these limping wounded, pursuing fitness beyond the threshold of pain. Running is an obsession for many of us—sometimes under control and sometimes not.

Injuries are only the grimmest results of a groping and stumbling understanding of running and training principles. There are also innumerable frustrations experienced by those who are stuck at plateaus they cannot pass, or by runners who follow some training routine to prepare for a ten-mile race or a marathon but end up disappointed and mystified at the results. Many of these runners are thwarted because they have only the vaguest understanding of what they are doing in their training.

Injuries tend to plague elite runners more than they do groups of more modest aspirations. This results partly from the necessity for world-class competitors to push close to the breakdown point to reach the highest level of conditioning, but it is also due to the same delusions that affect less talented runners. The rumors of blood doping* that made the rounds of the athletic world following Lasse Viren's second double-gold-medal performance at the 1976 Olympic Games (Viren won the 5000- and 10,000-meter races in both 1972 and 1976) demonstrated that many of the world's best runners and coaches still do not understand the principle of peaking. The evidence cited against Viren was that he did not do well in races before and after the Olympics, and many inferred from this that he had used blood doping to win. What Viren really did was to

---

*Blood doping is a method of increasing an athlete's red corpuscle count by giving him a transfusion of his own blood just before a competition. The blood is removed several weeks earlier and kept in cold storage until it is used. The idea is that oxygen transport may be improved by the greater volume of red blood cells, but it is equally possible that it might be reduced by increased viscosity of the blood. The whole question is largely conjectural, since no controlled experiments have ever been reported and no athletes are known to have used the procedure.

aim his training carefully at the races he really wanted to win, rather than wasting his best performances on races of minimal importance. The point is not that everyone should try to use this sort of peaking strategy, but that peaking is such a fundamental aspect of training that the reason for Viren's superb performances should have been obvious. The fact that they were misinterpreted demonstrates a real lack of understanding of fundamentals even among many of our best runners and coaches.

RUNNING BARRIERS

Only a few other sports are as firmly centered on the individual as running. There are team events and scoring in organized running competition, but even these are essentially the sum of individual performances rather than true team efforts like basketball or hockey. Tactics and strategy are important in racing, but they are not comparable to those of tennis, where each player's actions are dependent on those of the opponent. Strategy and tactics are not the essence of running but the fine points that decide a closely contested race. Even some strategic considerations have more to do with personal pacing than with the actions of other contestants. This is particularly true with long-distance events run on the roads. In a 1500-meter race a wily runner may be able to make a strategic break that boxes an opponent into a disadvantageous spot, but this would be extremely unlikely to work in a marathon, where rivalries center almost completely on wind advantages and psychological games designed to upset an opponent's pacing, confidence, or will. It is perfectly possible for a long-distance runner to compete in a race using a personal pacing strategy and ignoring the competition entirely, a tactic that would obviously be impossible in a handball game. Most running, in fact, is not competitive at all, and many runners either don't run races or don't take them very seriously. Even the dedicated racer will put in many training miles for every mile raced, and the meaning that he or she finds in the sport is more likely to be found in those daily runs than in the occasional races.

Both the satisfactions and frustrations of running are thus intensely personal. Many of the pleasures and agencies of particular efforts may be shared with friends: pacing one another in a good performance, sharing a beautiful sunrise, or helping one another through wintry morning training runs in slush and ice. But the physical exultation of running as you come into peak form and the depression of working through an injury or a stale period are both strictly your own. Most of the satisfactions and the difficulties of running can be shared only in a limited way. The best and the worst features of running flow equally from its solitary nature. It can be a selfish sport, demanding thousands of hours of training away from family, social demands, and other activities. This discipline can be as demanding and time-consuming for the middle-aged runner pursuing personal goals as for the Olympic contender. But it can bring with it a sense of satisfaction and equanimity that reflect back on other pursuits, especially in a society that often leaves people with little time to reflect and find personal balance.

The barriers in running are individual as well, and much of the long-term satisfaction of the dedicated runner comes from overcoming them. For most of us, there is little chance of winning a major race or of setting new world records, but the satisfaction of overcoming limitations that once seemed insurmountable can be at least as rewarding. Even for the serious competitor, the barriers in one's own mind are frequently more difficult to surmount than purely physical challenges, and the victories they provide are more lasting.

The much-touted barrier encountered by the marathon or ultramarathon runner around 20 miles, when muscle glycogen supplies are drained, is not the only "wall" to consider. The prescription for breaking through that particular wall is easy to formulate: the right kind of training, enough mileage correctly spaced, and proper pacing, all neatly written out in columns. The most difficult walls for the runner to scale, however, are those in the mind, particularly the ones erected by inadequate understanding of the limitations and capacities of the body.

The aim of this book is to help the reader to work through some of those barriers. The main reason for drawing on the research and personal experimentation that has been done in serious competitive running is to shed light on problems faced by many dedicated runners, whether they are interested in racing or not. The wall of marathon fame is as massive for the runner trying to break 4½ hours as for the one pressing for 2½, and the solutions in training techniques are virtually the same. Peaking and stale periods are not phenomena confined to world-class runners; they occur in the experience of 8-minute-per-mile runners as well, and learning how to control them can be just as important.

THE INJURY CYCLE AND HOW TO BREAK IT

There are many causes of running injuries, and the subject is a complicated one. Some specific problems are discussed in Chapter XIV of this book, together with techniques for preventing and treating injuries. They are covered in more detail in my book *Running Without Pain* (Dial Press, 1980). The most frequent cause of injuries, however, fits better into the topic of running barriers than into discussions of foot pronation or stretching exercises. An alarming number of runners are pushing themselves into serious injuries, sometimes permanent ones, as a result of a misguided drive that outstrips their understanding of the sport. They ignore pain and the often repeated advice to work up to long distances gradually, and continue hobbling out their weekly mileage until they are literally crippled.

The group that seems to be most prone to this sort of insanity is that of male runners in their late twenties to early forties. Some are already quite fit when they begin running, so that they progress to a reasonably strong level very quickly. Others have been running for a period of six months to a couple of years to reach a similar level of fitness, but then fall into the same syndrome of impatience. Women and men in other age groups are not immune, but men entering or approaching middle age seem the most vulnerable to delusions of grandeur and invulnerability that are poorly matched with their real physical capacity to absorb abuse.

The syndrome seems to repeat itself again and again. One acquaintance of mine will serve as an example. He is physically very strong and in excellent condition from active participation in a variety of sports. He took up running and rapidly became enthusiastic about the benefits. Within a few months he was aiming at a marathon only about eight weeks away and running forty miles a week. This was probably more training than his body was ready to tolerate after a short period of running, especially since he is heavily muscled and has a large frame, so that his legs and joints take a good deal of pounding as he runs. At the same time, this was not nearly enough training to allow him to safely run a marathon at a good pace. It might have been fine if he had been content to jog the distance at a moderate rate, but that is not really in his nature. I suspect that his legs hurt through most of his training runs; otherwise he probably would have put in still more mileage.

Our complusive friend finished his marathon in fairly good time, considering his level of conditioning, his face contorted with pain. Soon afterward he entered another demanding race, a 21-mile mountain race with a long downhill grade following a steep climb. Again he pushed himself through the pain barrier. Before long he could scarcely walk, having to descend stairs backward. He called a mutual friend and asked whether a puffy feeling was normal when a finger was pushed behind the kneecap. His friend gently advised him to see a doctor. The poor fellow received some bad medical advice, undoubtedly compounded by his own drive to return to running, but the upshot after still more heavy training was permanent and probably irreparable damage to his knee.

This is an extreme example, but it follows an all-too-familiar pattern that is becoming more and more common among middle-level runners. The ambition of dedicated runners often exceeds the ability, and training is piled on faster than aching joints and tendons can adapt. Sooner or later the inevitable breakdown occurs, and the runner begins the round of trying various shoes, different podiatrists, bee pollen, or any other miracle cure making the rounds—anything but the patience and slow building-up that will allow the body to adapt to the stresses of speed and distance.

Indeed, running may be one of the best examples of the human capacity for self-delusion. We can all recognize the symptoms of overuse and overtraining in others, but many of us seem incapable of seeing it in ourselves, at least until we have had a painful lesson or two. I remember going through this syndrome myself, running a long hill every morning with poorly designed shoes as my Achilles tendonitis got progressively worse. It was clear from my difficulties that something was wrong, but I convinced myself for some time that the injury was stable and not being worsened by my running. Obviously, somewhere between the time that the tendon trouble began to manifest itself in a mild way and the time when I could scarcely walk, something got worse; but it did so incrementally, with no dramatic changes from day to day. Fortunately, I learned my lesson from this one episode, as some do not. Wiser runners, however, will profit from the difficulties of others, rather than insisting on making the mistakes themselves.

Nor are serious competitive runners immune to this syndrome, a fact that is apparent to anyone who has followed the careers of very many long- or middle-distance athletes. Again and again one finds the pattern of injury striking the athlete at his or her peak. Such injuries are partly due to the fine line that the best competitors have to run in order to reach their best form without overtraining and breaking down. A slight miscalculation can result in serious injury for the top level runner. The injuries experienced by world-class athletes are not always the result of the inherent risks of the highest grade of training, however. The best athletes seem to be as vulnerable to the delusions of invincibility as are their less talented fellow runners. They are often as reluctant as the rest of us to heed the warning signs of overtraining. Some of the best marathoners in the world have been laid low by trying to compete again and again before completely healing from an earlier injury.

Like attempts to move too quickly to a more serious level of running, the effort to come off an injury too fast is a primary cause of more serious injuries. After the frustrations of injury there is a desperate impulse to make up for lost time by training extra hard. This can be a disastrous error, both because the injury has to have time to heal and because some deconditioning will have taken place, so that the muscles have to be built up and stretched to full length before being subjected to hard training. The runner may be able to run through many injuries while healing progresses simultaneously, but only if extreme care is exercised to avoid overdoing things. In the case of some injuries, like torn tendons, complete rest is necessary, together with stretching, until the healing process is well under way.

Despite the importance of foot supports and other corrective measures for some runners, I am convinced that the primary cause of injuries is improper training, including failure to warm up and stretch adequately. This is particularly true for experienced runners, since people with the worst mechanical problems either stop running at an early stage or seek out corrective aids. It is also especially true for older runners, who both heal and adapt to training more slowly, so that they suffer more for their abuses than do younger athletes.

Simply describing the usual injury syndrome, of course, implicitly prescribes the primary rule for prevention: *Don't overdo it.* But the fact that so many runners have ignored this precept in the past demonstrates that the statement of the problem is not enough in itself. By its nature, running involves pushing back the limits of what we think is possible, driving ourselves farther than we ever thought we could go. This kind of self-imposed challenge does not mix well with self-restraint, and when you are actually training it can be difficult to distinguish between healthy stress and unhealthy strain.

Most of the time, the real key to injury prevention lies in good training, and the runner who genuinely understands this fact is not likely to be seriously hurt. This is true partly because a training program that is well designed for the individual to get good results by increasing speed and endurance as efficiently as possible is also well designed to prevent injuries. Proper timing of speed work, good base training, and adequate rest are as important to tuning up the body to run well as they are to preventing injuries. Inadequate rest, intervals run frequently at the wrong time, and similar errors result in erratic performances and frustrating lack of progress, as well as in injuries. Rational planning of your training will probably keep you healthy and pain-free, and it is also the most reliable way to achieve good performance and to enjoy your running to the fullest.

MOVING ON

For the beginner, the simple act of running a mile, then two, then five, is a satisfying achievement, perhaps followed by the conquest of a few personal time barriers. The efforts put forward by the novice are great, but the rewards are obvious and come with satisfying rapidity. For the experienced and serious runner this is often not the case. The dedicated runner has an easier time in many ways, because running has become fairly easy and truly enjoyable and because the runner knows his or her own abilities rather well. But there are also difficulties. Achieving clear improvement becomes harder and takes much longer once you are already in fairly good condition. The days of seeing major progress from week to week are gone, and every runner seems to reach a stage periodically where the body refuses to get stronger. The length of time required for major conditioning changes to take place makes training choices harder, too, because the feedback from the body returns so slowly that we are not always sure whether a particular training routine is good, bad, or indifferent. This is one reason why careful thought about training goals and techniques is so crucial for the dedicated runner who wants to continue to improve.

Probably the most useful step in making progress is to set yourself a definite goal toward which to work. Vague aspirations to become more fit are fine for the beginner; but particularly for the runner who is stuck at a plateau, it is important to have a specific target on which to focus your training. Such a goal provides an incentive to follow your training schedule and avoid disruptive interruptions. It also will allow you to work out an exact schedule, designed to accomplish a specific purpose—to run a first marathon, to run ten miles in a particular time, to win in your age group at a particular race, or whatever.

Working out a training schedule for a particular purpose serves as a check on the goal as well. If you do a good job of scheduling your training, you will also be checking the feasibility of the objective. It may soon become apparent that you have set your sights either too high or too low, in which case the goal needs to be changed. For most of us, the objective itself is arbitrary, anyway; what is important is not so much whether we run a 2:40 marathon or a 2:45, but the sense of accomplishment that comes from a disciplined attempt and the pleasure of the running along the way. For serious competitors, of course, victory or loss may be far more important. Even for them, however, the experiences en route are likely to become more meaningful in hindsight as the years go by. Most of us, having started running far too late to have delusions of Olympic gold or Boston Marathon victories, don't have to worry about such problems. Satisfaction for us is of a more modest kind, but can be anticipated with far more certainty of realization.

The mechanics of working out a training schedule will be discussed after the elements of training have been covered in more detail, but it is worth giving a brief overview here. I think that long-term cycles of training, rather like the traditional competitive schedules, fit in well with the natural rhythms of the body. Whether or not you are training for a particular race or season, the body seems to adapt most readily to reaching a peak of fitness for a month or six weeks, followed by a period of more moderate effort. This does not mean that you should stop running, but rather that you should accept some ebb and flow in your efforts, rather than reaching a peak and then expecting to drive up from that pinnacle to a new high. A more natural progression to a higher peak is to drop down a little to a slightly lower plateau and move along a steady level for a time before making an effort to reach a greater height of fitness.

Thus the mode of training that this book stresses relies on a large amount of base training over long distances at considerably less than maximum effort. Some base running may be done at good speeds, and this type of training will slowly increase the average pace of most runners. Some *fartlek* (training at mixed speeds with occasional dashes when you feel like it) and hill training may be included, and many runners like to use a little speed work or intervals occasionally. The main point is one of emphasis. During base training you should not concern yourself very much about speed or make any concerted efforts to improve it. The object of base training is to develop stamina, cardiovascular conditioning, and mechanical strength in your joints, tendons, and ligaments. Base conditioning provides the underlying foundation for the concentrated speed work that brings on peak fitness and performance. Too much really hard training or racing with an inadequate base will bring on a minor peak and then a spell of doldrums. By trying to work even harder, the flagging runner is likely to be hurt and certainly will not improve. Base conditioning is the running that builds up your strength and makes you feel good. It makes up most of the running diet for everyone from the round-the-block jogger to the serious competitor. A runner interested mainly in fitness may never try to make faster, all-out efforts using base training as a platform. You can race perfectly happily and safely without peaking if you are doing regular base running of this type.

For serious racing, however, or to run for your own satisfaction at the strongest level possible for you, it is necessary to increase your strength and leg speed. Efficient running at any speed requires that the leg muscles be trained at that speed, so that the nerves and motor units function together efficiently. Most important, you have to learn to relax at the pace you want to run, whether the race is short or long. You can train yourself to relax while running hard only by doing a lot of practice running at high speed.

Intensive work on strength can either be combined with base training when you are already in fairly good shape, or used following base training as part of the peaking procedure. Hill training, rough trail running, and running in sand are some of the best ways of building strength. This additional strength helps to build reserves for interval and tempo work, and it helps keep you from tiring and tensing up during long races.

But the essential ingredient that must be added to your base training if you want to reach peak form is speed work, discussed at length in later chapters of this book. There are several types of speed training, and a carefully thought-out mixture of these is most efficient. If you have done your background training, you will be able to take on a heavy diet of speed work without seriously risking injury, providing you maintain your common sense and make sure to stretch and warm up adequately before running hard. Runners vary a good deal in the length of time they need to develop maximum leg speed, and nothing but experience will tell you how long you need. Generally, about a month of hard work will bring you up to peak form, but some runners are fast after a couple of weeks of speed training, while others require six or seven weeks to peak.

Speed work should build up slowly, like everything in running, and there may be no apparent results for a couple of weeks. A heavy dose of interval training is usually the most important form of speed work. Intervals consist of fast running for a short distance, followed by a similar spell of walking or jogging, repeated with variations many times. The idea is that the runner can train at race pace or faster for considerable distances, without experiencing the acute lactic-acid buildup and fatigue in the muscles that would develop if this distance were run in one long stretch. More work can therefore be concentrated into each training session.

It is important to realize that the top speed that is built up in a hard, intensive training push like this cannot be maintained forever, particularly if you race regularly. Races run at a fast pace drain a lot of the body's resources, and this is particularly true of long races. If you think of your base training as putting money in the bank, racing corresponds to spending it. The deeper you dig into your reserves, the more time you will have to spend building them back up. This subject is discussed at length later in the book, but the concept is critical. The idea is to bring yourself to peak form for the races you really want to win or for the period when you want to be most fit. After a while you should drop back somewhat so that you don't put too much of a strain on your body, go stale, or get hurt.

This concept of peaking is important even for runners who never run races. Certain training routines will bring you up to peak condition, and if you have put really concentrated effort into your training, you should expect to drop back after a month or two. You'll get the most fun out of your running if you work with your body's natural rhythm instead of resisting it.

KEEPING A TRAINING DIARY

In order to make your training come together, it is important to keep track of where you have been. Memory is naturally selective, retaining a few good runs, a few bad ones, and some that were notable for reasons you may not even be able to define. You might remember a year later that your fastest time over a particular training run was 68:23, but you are not likely to be able to pick out all the details before and after to serve as a guide to your current training effort. Was this performance only one of a whole series that were almost equally fast, or did it follow lots of runs that were ten minutes slower? How much mileage were you doing at the time? Had you been doing speed work or a lot of hill running? These are the details that should

guide you to a more intelligent refinement of your training
next year. If you go back over your training diary occasionally,
patterns will start to emerge.

Relying on memory or a sloppy record for this sort of information is a great way either to become discouraged or to de-
lude yourself with wishful thinking. You are likely to forget
how much training went into the good marathon performance
you had last year and try to repeat it with inadequate preparation. A look at your diary could tell you either to pass up a race
you are contemplating or to set your sights lower.

People have many ways of keeping track of what they do:
charts, little black books, or notes on a calendar will serve
equally well, so long as you keep careful records and put down
all the necessary information. You don't need a daily record of
exact distances, splits, and total times, though some people
keep all this data. Personally, I find that too fixed an obsession
with times and pace is bad for my running. I'd rather not compare my exact pace, time, and distance every day. Such comparison tempts one to try to go faster each run, a routine that is
soon self-defeating.

Usually people have a number of regular runs that they do
on different days. I like to describe a route in detail somewhere
in the diary, so that if I am no longer doing it three years later
I can refer back and find out just what I meant by the "Three
Saddles Run" or the "Shanahan Circuit." Then I simply name
the run I made on a particular day, giving a subjective descrip-
tion of how hard I worked at it, whether it felt fast or slow, and
the elapsed time if I bothered to record it. As a rule experienced runners have a pretty good idea of the pace and distance
they run on a given day, whether a course has been accurately
measured or not, so it isn't hard to keep a fairly close record of
weekly mileage. You may not know whether you are running at
6:10 or 6:15, but you can usually tell that it's neither a 5- nor a
7-minute mile.

If you are still not a good enough judge of pace to be able to
estimate the length of your runs, it is worth making occasional
runs on a track or a measured course to give yourself a basis of

comparison. Thus, if you run a measured six-mile course at moderate effort in forty-five minutes, an hour run at about the same pace over an equivalent sampling of hills must be close to eight miles long. For the purposes of your diary, noting that you ran eight miles at moderate effort is fine, except when you're trying to work on exact pacing. The stopwatch routine can be saved for periods of speed work.

You can keep your main records in terms of either time or mileage, but I much prefer mileage. Some people find they put less pressure on themselves if they keep track of time; that's fine if you prefer to do it that way. The two are not directly convertible, however, as some have suggested. In figuring out the training distances required for particular races using the formulas on pages 146–9, you should convert to approximate distance, taking into account the pace at which you are training.

In recording race times and interval sessions, you should be as accurate as possible. These times are the ones that tell you how to interpret everything else, and they are more directly comparable, since you will normally try fairly hard in a race or a serious interval session. If you actually go out and run a course for time, record it accurately. Wishful thinking will merely disappoint you later on when you are faster, since you will look back in your diary and find times recorded that are imprecise.

HAVING FUN

One of the advantages of becoming a really confirmed runner is that you keep going with sufficient regularity to avoid the misery of having to climb back up into shape. Running is most enjoyable when you are always in good enough condition to go out and enjoy ten miles on the trails or the roads. Nearly all of us go through cycles where we are in better or worse shape, depending on the demands of work and family or the depredations of a vacation with more lolling around and beer drinking than running. "Good" and "bad" conditions are relative, though, and if you are lucky or smart, you'll avoid sinking too far out of shape.

It is easy to take running too seriously, however, and we all need a bit of perspective injected occasionally. You can't stay in training without trying hard, and all runners who have been doing consistently good mileage for some time have learned that the dedication is worthwhile. From time to time, however, it is a good idea to remind yourself that running is a part of life, not life itself. When you come home from a party and realize that you have talked about nothing but running the whole time; when you spouse or roommate is so sick of hearing about marathon training and pacing that he or she is ready to scream; and when you are no longer enjoying your runs because you are working so hard to make sure that you get them all in—step back and have a good laugh at yourself! This is supposed to be fun! You'll keep running longer and probably do better if you remember to have a good time along the way. That's what running is all about.

CHAPTER II

THE GATE AT FIVE MILES:

Notes for the Intermediate Runner

THIS CHAPTER IS intended for runners who are averaging at least two miles a day, but rarely run five or more. Those regularly averaging in excess of thirty-five miles per week will probably want to skip to the next chapter. Some runners and joggers are perfectly happy with modest distances, usually as a form of aerobic exercise to maintain general fitness. Whatever their original intentions, however, many people end up jogging a couple of miles a day only during a transition stage before either going on to longer runs or gradually giving up the activity. Some fail to try running longer distances because they find their two- or three-mile runs rather boring and a joyless chore at best.

It is a real mistake to drop running just because you don't find distances of two or three miles to be pleasant. Many avid distance runners have had exactly the same experience and still dislike short runs. I often don't start to enjoy a run until I have been out on the road for a few miles and my body has had time to increase circulation and otherwise adjust to the energy de-

mands of running. This is particularly true of early morning
runs, when the transition from sleep is being made as well.
After a few miles, the blood starts to course through your veins
easily, your muscles have warmed up, the joints are lubricated,
and the body machinery starts to function happily. This is
when running really becomes enjoyable for most of the serious
runners I know; the first couple of miles are run without much
interest, in the knowledge that the experience will be more
pleasant later on in the run. Of course there are days when everything feels great from the very beginning of the run, even
early in the morning; but it is important for people who don't
usually run farther than a couple of miles to know that this is
often not true even for people who regularly put in twelve or
fourteen miles a day.

For the runner of modest experience, I think that there is a
major transition point that occurs at about the time daily mileage passes five miles. The dropout rate in running is far higher
among people who never get to this stage. Part of the reason is
obviously that a certain amount of conditioning and commitment is required just to reach this point, and those who get
beyond five miles a day obviously have both qualities. I think
that there is an even more important reason, though. Personally, I never liked running much and had a generally negative feeling about it even some time after I had started to run
regularly. I ran because I became convinced that it was an efficient conditioning exercise, and I didn't have the time in my
schedule to train in ways that I liked better with enough regularity.

At about the time I started to regularly exceed five miles of
running a day, my viewpoint changed, and I started to really
enjoy my running. It felt good, and I found myself savoring the
motion, speeding up my tempo on a level stretch after a steep
hill just for the pleasure of the sport, looking forward to long
runs through the countryside. In talking with other runners
and querying them on the subject, I found that the vast majority had had the same sort of experience. There are natural runners who have always delighted in running at any distance, but

most people in our society really seem to get physical and mental pleasure from the activity itself (as opposed to its tangible benefits) only after they have begun running about five miles a day. In my unscientific sampling, I have been amazed at the high percentage of regular runners who have had the same feelings.

It is at these longer distances that you experience elation with the act of running—the much-touted runner's high, holistic experience, or whatever you wish to call it. The sense of running is different and more positive in any case, and probably these borrowed terms are not particularly descriptive. The experiences of distance runners during their most enjoyable long runs flow directly out of the physical activity. There is a natural pleasure in motion once the body has reached a stable state of energy output, and this is greatly increased when your body is used to long runs, so that you feel in easy control of a flowing movement. Your mind relaxes and is free to wander, but at the same time there is a feeling of unity with the body. It is interesting that in this mental state, you will sometimes be aware only of your movement, at other times of the changing scenery around, and often of nothing at all. Yet frequently in this resting state, you will suddenly come up with the solution to a problem in your daily life that you may have been working on for weeks.

Enough rhapsodic pages have been written about the joys of running, so I will not bore the reader with still more. And running is often just plain hard work. The main point here is that the pleasurable aspects of running are typically encountered after the runner has passed a certain mileage threshold in daily average. Even then during any particular run it is after the first couple of miles of warming up that the runner usually really begins to enjoy the running.

For the intermediate runner who has passed the initial difficulties of the novice, it follows that the next barrier is likely to be getting up to somewhere around thirty to thirty-five miles a week. The primary obstacle for many runners is a psychological one: They may enjoy the healthful effects of running, but it doesn't give them a lot of pleasure when they are actually doing it. Thus, there is little incentive to go any farther in a day. For intermediate runners, going farther may also require significant commitments of time, because they are often running at slower speeds than runners who put in more extensive mileage. Additional mileage increments are likely to slow them down still more at first. It is particularly difficult to increase mileage if you are doing all the running you can within a limited time block—during a lunch hour, for example, or between the time you get home from work and the beginning of a family supper. Your boss might not be understanding if you started getting back a half-hour late every day, and your family is not likely to be enthusiastic about postponing supper until eight.

BITING OFF MORE THAN YOU CAN CHEW

When you make up your mind to push on past five miles a day, you have to start out by deciding where you should extend yourself first. There is a series of choices to be made in revising your schedule and pacing: Should you run faster, farther, more often, more steadily? Once you start thinking about the ways in which you could forge ahead, there is a natural tendency to decide to do everything.

Let's begin by quashing any quixotic impulses you may have to bite off more than anyone could chew by trying to improve in all areas at the same time. Runners naturally tend to be somewhat driven; after all, people who are perfectly complacent about their lives aren't likely to take up running in the first place. When we make up our minds to do something, it is natural to take on too much at once. Just as some people are likely to resolve to give up smoking, go on a diet, treat their families better, and so on, all on the same day, runners will vow to increase their daily mileage, regularity, and speed. This sort of determination is usually simply futile in daily life, since it rapidly dissolves under the acid test of reality. For runners, however, it can be dangerous, since many of us are strong willed and thickheaded enough to actually try to pull such a program off. The body's mechanisms for dealing with stress are discussed in more detail in subsequent chapters, but it is obvious that they can handle only limited extra stress at any given time. By increasing your body's workload in several areas at the same time, you will almost certainly overload your system. You'll probably get sore muscles after a few days, become chronically tired, and come down with the flu. Alternatively, you may develop an injury in one of your legs that puts an end to your excesses.

Though you may occasionally want to run both fast and far on a particular day, you should increase the overall stress on your body slowly and in only one area at a time. If you are running only three days a week now, for example, doing your four miles a day, don't increase to five or six days a week and go up to five miles a day at the same time. You should do just the opposite; if you are appreciably increasing your overall mileage and time, let up a little on both your pace and your daily average until your body has had a chance to get used to the new workload. Then increase one of the other factors. This step-by-step approach is crucial in making training progress.

One of the difficult facts to which you must learn to resign yourself as you progress is that the reaction time of the body to conditioning is slow, especially when you want to make permanent improvements. It is important to learn that the body has a whole series of interconnected physical rhythms in response to training. Since we are always pleased to see progress and would just as soon ignore regression, we often act as though short-term gains were really major steps forward. The key to long-term progress at the intermediate level of running is actually to *avoid* pushing the body into temporary peaks. Raising the intensity of training too quickly can do just that, giving you good performances the next week and poor ones for the following month or six weeks. Since the same pattern occurs in different ways for world-class runners, one of the most valuable lessons you can assimilate early in your running career is to train with a long view in mind and to realize when you have pushed too hard and brought on a temporary peak that it probably won't last. Don't be disappointed when the doldrums strike afterward; they will pass, too.

HARD/EASY SCHEDULES

There are sound physiological arguments for running one day and resting the next, discussed in more detail in Chapter V. The easy day/hard day rhythm is well established as a training principle, because the body cannot recover completely from a hard training session in twenty-four hours. But this does not necessarily mean that you should run only every other day if you want to make progress in running.

One reason for this lies in the joints, tendons, and ligaments of the body, which adapt much more slowly to increased training than the muscles do. They seem to increase in strength best under the stimulus of daily running. It does not appear to be possible to work your overall mileage very high unless you run on most days, because the skeletal structures start to protest; they are not up to the strain. The hard/easy route is essential, but most easy days should be easy *running* days rather than days off. As with all adjectives connected with running, "hard" and "easy" come to mean different things at varying levels of conditioning. For top-level marathoners, running twenty-five miles at seven minutes per mile is an easy training run taken on a day between hard speed-work sessions. For many of us, this would be a good performance in a race. For the intermediate runner, this may be a level of performance that is still far in the future. Thus, for the beginner, a two-mile run at any speed is likely to be a hard day, and the next day should be one of alternate walking and light jogging. For someone running four miles, three days a week, a good way to progress would be to add three-mile jogs on the intervening days.

I think that for intermediate runners who want to get better, it is important to start running at least five or six days a week. Personally, I prefer to try to run every day, unless I am doing some kind of hard training of another kind on the alternate days. There does not seem to be any substitute for the overall training stimulus provided by building up extensive mileage month in and month out. The distance that you can run at a good pace is more or less determined by the total mileage you run on a regular basis and it is simply not feasible for most people to build their mileage up very much by running only three days a week.

Another important factor is that intermediate runners who are running only a few days per week are likely to do so in an irregular pattern. The days are not usually evenly spaced, as a hard/easy regimen would require. Instead, a person is likely to run for a couple of days in a row, drop off for three or four days, train again for two or three days, and so on. This is certainly better than not training at all, but progress will soon drop off to nothing until a regular discipline is established.

The final reason for running on most days is simply the practical fact that it works. Except for a few athletes who train hard in other sports and who are actually active every day, I don't know of any good runners who don't run regularly on most days. This may be simply because we tend to stop altogether when we don't run as a matter of habit most of the time. Regardless of the reasons, however, as a practical matter people who plan to run only three days a week usually stop running completely after a while. Your schedule or lassitude may sometimes interfere and cause a setback, but if you want to run well, you should try to run at least five or six days a week.

STARTING TO RUN EVERY DAY

When you first start to run regularly six or seven days a week, you may want to reduce your daily mileage or speed somewhat. Whether this is necessary will depend on how much you have been running and how you feel as you go along. In any case, you shouldn't push hard for the first two or three weeks. Run at a relaxed pace, without worrying much about either mileage or speed, concentrating on getting out for a reasonable period each day, and reducing the distance covered if you have any hangover the next day—aching knees, tendon problems, and so on. (You should be stretching and doing supplementary exercises regularly and taking the usual precautions against injuries—see Chapter XIV.) If you don't feel the strain, you can then up the pace or mileage, but be sure to wait a couple of weeks before making a judgment if you have suddenly gone from three days a week to six or seven.

At this stage you can leave the hard/easy routine pretty much up to the way you feel—just don't push too hard, particularly if your legs ache or on a day when you feel somewhat off form even after you have run a mile or two. The cautions throughout the rest of the book against overtraining apply to intermediate runners as much as to hotshots. You may have to work gradually up to running every day, alternating running one day with walking and jogging the next whenever you begin to show signs of overstress. Remember that if you take the same daily run when you start running seven days a week as you did when you ran three, you will be more than doubling your mileage, and this can require several months to allow your body to accommodate to the extra workload.

WORKING OUT A ROUTINE

One key factor in running every day is to make it a regular part of your daily routine, finding some particular period during the day when you can run and regularly going out at that time. The hour might be different on Mondays than on Wednesdays if you have a difficult schedule; but if you have a definite time allocated and make a point of going out then, you'll be far more likely to be regular than you are if you just work your running in when the chance arises. On many days, the opportunity just won't arise unless it is preplanned, like going to work or any other daily necessity.

Most people who run lead busy lives, and it is often tempting to assign running to some block of time that may not work out as a practical matter. Lunchtime running is ideal for quite a few people, but for many of us it is unrealistic; other engagements come up that can't be avoided, and the run is never taken. If you miss your run more than once a week, replan your schedule to pick a more realistic time. Many of us get stuck running early in the mornings, simply because no other time of day is really feasible.

Once you have worked out a realistic schedule, stick to it, rain or shine. The hardest part of any run is getting out the door. Most dedicated runners enjoy the run once they have gotten started. Even those who look forward to it throughout the day sometimes find excuses not to get out when they should. Normal human inertia works against you unless you make it a rule *always* to take your run. On one day it will be snowing outside; on another you have to finish a report. Once you have established a firm running routine, however, the inertia works in your favor, and most regular runners find that their daily runs make them more efficient in other pursuits, rather than robbing them of valuable time.

DISTANCE VS. SPEED

Once you are running regularly at least five days a week, preferably six or seven, the inevitable training question is whether you should run farther or faster as your next step in training. It is important to mention once again the caution against trying to pile on extra stress too quickly. If you have just started running five miles a day for six days a week instead of three, you have already increased your overall distance enormously and should not impose any additional strain on your body until you have had plenty of time to adjust.

After you are getting out as a matter of habit on most days, the question of distance or speed revolves around your current performance. If you are running less than five miles a day at speeds usually faster than nine minutes per mile, I would recommend that you gradually increase your average distance up to *at least* forty miles a week before worrying about speed at all. Actually, at this level of running experience, most people find that their speed and distance slowly increase together, except when they are adding mileage rather rapidly. It is particularly risky when you are running only three or four miles a day after engaging in the sport for a relatively short period to try to increase your speed if you are already doing eight-minute miles or better. High-school track runners may get away with this; forty-year-old office workers generally won't. Even in high school and college track, a lot of fast running over a short distance without a distance background used to take a heavy toll of injured athletes. These days extensive distance training is standard, so most young competitors have a better distance foundation on which to build.

One way to handle the distance vs. speed problem is to concentrate on the time you run each day. If you average between an hour and an hour and a half per day, working fairly hard on some days and relaxing on others, the distance and speed will gradually take care of themselves without a great deal of thought on your part. You may do a longer period one day and a shorter one the next to make up a hard/easy routine, or simply go slow for a couple of days and fast on the third. Naturally, you may need to make some adjustments of your running routes so that your timing works out, but you will soon learn which route requires eighty minutes or so on a fast day and which one is right for an easy day. Runners who are still at a lower performance level can use this same routine by simply alternating walking and running for the chosen period, with more running on the hard days and more walking on the easy ones.

Thus, if you are now running 40 miles a week, averaging 10 minutes or so a mile by running about 6 miles each day in an hour or so, you might begin by increasing your time to 75–90 minutes, not making any particular attempt to pick up speed, but letting the pace take care of itself. You may want to slow down on some days at first, to make up for the increased time on the roads. After a month or more, when you are sure your body is adjusted to the inevitable increase in mileage, try putting more effort into the run two or three times a week. Don't do any real speed work. Just make sure that your effort stays up through your entire run. Once you have been running at good effort three days a week for a while, try introducing one relaxed longer run of 2½–3 hours one day a week. By maintaining this routine over a period of time, backing off whenever your body shows signs of overstress, I think you will find both your overall speed and your distance increasing steadily. If you are running for 75 minutes or so a day, you will probably begin by finding that on your fast days you are covering 8 miles or a little more, while on the slow ones you manage only 6 or so. As you improve, these distances will increase progressively, and your pace will go up along with them. As you get over 50 or 60 miles a week, with at least some of your *distance* runs accomplished at eight-minute miles or better, you will have moved into normal base training for the distance runner. The later chapters of this book discuss training programs from this stage on.

TIMING AND MEASUREMENT

In the last chapter I strongly recommended keeping a careful training diary. This is particularly important for the intermediate runner. A runner without a great deal of experience in judging time, distances, and general performance will not be able to make any reasonable comparison of his or her situation from month to month without some fairly detailed record. An experienced racer will at least have the results of particular races to compare, while the intermediate runner has no equivalent data.

It is not necessary to have accurate records of pace and distance for every day's run, however, so you don't need to do your runs around a quarter-mile track or time them with a stopwatch. The intermediate runner is far better off avoiding day-to-day comparisons of exact pace, distance, and so on. What is needed is enough information to provide meaningful comparisons if you look back at your diary six months later. Thus, you will probably have a number of regular running courses, and if you mention in your diary that you ran a particular one at a moderate pace (subjective descriptions of effort are fine if you keep them personally consistent) in about 1½ hours, you will know if you are at the same general level three months later or if you have progressed significantly.

You can complete your record so that it will be useful in later years by doing an occasional training run on a track or a measured course and carrying a watch to note how long it takes you to run six, ten, or fifteen miles. A regular watch may not be adequate for 220-yard intervals, but it is fine for ordinary training runs of a few miles or more. If you have a record that in a given month you ran a hard 10 miles in 73 minutes, you will know that your standard for a hard training pace at the time was about 7:18 per mile. Next year you will be able to make appropriate allowances in interpreting the rest of your diary when your standard has improved to 6:05's or slipped to 8:15's. This will be important, because in trying to work for a new goal of an ultradistance run or a better time in a marathon, the other notes in your diary will be helpful only if you have a basis for comparison. On the other hand, making detailed measurements of time and distance every day at this stage of your training will only lead to a dangerous and boring obsession with numbers, while contributing nothing to your later understanding.

MOVING THROUGH THE GATE

Extending your regular training mileage beyond 30 or 35 miles a week is one of the most exciting progressions in running, comparable to the surge in fitness that you feel as a novice early in your running career. As you pass through the five-mile-a-day barrier, all sorts of possibilities in running begin to open up. You begin to realize that you can run a marathon, do regular ten-mile races simply as a matter of routine, and go for weekend trail runs lasting for several hours—and that you can enjoy doing it! I think that you will find that it is one of the best experiences in running.

CHAPTER III

MOVING ON:

*Racing, Training,
and Running for Fun*

As DEDICATED RUNNERS we are as full of contradictions and conflicting feelings about our sport as we are about other enterprises in life that we take seriously. Some of the ambiguities about running arise from the nature of the activity, while others are outgrowths of our own ambivalence. Running gives us feelings of relaxation and personal freedom, yet these result only from rigorous adherence to a routine involving a lot of hard work. Many runners are generally repelled by the competitive aspects of our society. They take up running to escape competition in other areas of life and then deliberately seek out competition in running. Still others claim to be completely uncompetitive about running, yet both their training schedules and the way they run belie the contention.

Inconsistencies like these are certainly not confined to running. Virtually all important aspects of our lives include similar crosscurrents. We do sometimes carry inappropriate conflicts into activities like primarily recreational running, however. Individuals who are compulsive and driven in their work often

29

tend to apply the same habits to running. For middle-aged beginners, this sort of compulsive behavior may be just what is needed to get through the difficult problems faced by the novice runner. Later on, however, this kind of habit often drives the runner into working too hard at the sport instead of progressing naturally. At the same time, it is likely to drain much of the pleasure from the activity.

Runners who are serious contenders for national or international honors inevitably have to balance a far wider range of objectives, worldly aspirations, and compromises than most of us. Whatever the athlete's individual motivations, the glory and difficulty of the upper reaches of the sport are inevitably fraught with complications. This is normal in human endeavors that have important consequences for a lot of people. The politics, sacrifices, and difficult personal and group decisions are unavoidable. For most of us, however, there is simply no possibility of competing and winning against world-class runners. We don't have to decide whether the risks, the sacrifices, and the compromises are justified by the chance of a national record or of Olympic gold. We'll be lucky to win in our own age class in a local marathon, a thoroughly satisfying personal achievement, but hardly one of earth-shattering significance.

Those of us without Olympic aspirations ought to be able to retain our sense of proportion about running and to remember our real goals in the sport. Whatever the attractions of a particular ten-mile race, the Boston Marathon, or a personal record around a favorite course, the aspects of running that are really important to most of us are the feelings of health and relaxation that we obtain both from individual runs and from regular strenuous exercise, the prospects of retaining some vigor into old age, and the satisfaction of looking forward to many future runs. Set in this perspective, the need for straining beyond reason to break a particular time barrier *this month* or *in this race* can be seen in a more reasonable light. A little drive toward short-term goals is a good thing, providing that it does not interfere with more important long-range objectives or become so obsessive that the fun goes out of the sport.

Running ought to be fun. In its essence it is play or recreation; the competitive aspects and drive toward better performances should be subordinated to an overall pleasure in the sport, rather than the other way around. The painful push at the end of a hard workout or at the finish of a race can be fun, but running through pain every morning is not. In the long run, by keeping your sense of perspective you will maintain your interest in running, and you are more likely to improve steadily over the years. Most important, running will continue to nourish you physically and psychologically, rather than becoming a destructive obsession.

SETTING GOALS

Besides the long-term goals of improving fitness and enjoyment over the years, it is often pleasant and helpful to work toward more immediate objectives. At some stage, however, you are likely to find yourself at a flat spot in your running, wanting to improve or to explore some new side of the sport. Continuing your regular running will usually bring additional progress, but there are times when you seem to be in a permanent slump.

Often the best way to make long-term gains is to work toward some more immediate goal: a marathon next summer, an extended mountain run, a traverse of the Grand Canyon, or simply a magical time barrier at a particular distance. Most commonly, distance runners center their goals around a particular race—breaking a time barrier in a marathon is the most popular objective. Just running a marathon and finishing is often the target for the less experienced runner, but even in this case a time goal is implicit. Given a long enough period, after all, you could walk the marathon distance on your knees. To be meaningful the race has to be *run* at a pace involving some challenge for the particular contestant.

For those who have not yet run a marathon at all or who have not run enough of them to have become blasé about the distance, the marathon provides an excellent goal. It is long enough to give you the incentive to do all the training you can tolerate, but it is an objective that is within the reach of any healthy individual. If you have already run one or more marathons, improving your time presents an impressively intricate training problem, and the commitment of the distance is sufficient so that preparation will require many months. Marathons have become so popular that it is easy to find one that just suits nearly any schedule you arrange. There is also a guarantee that if things go awry and you fail to quite meet your training goals, there will be another marathon in which you can compete when you are ready. Ultramarathons and races like Pike's Peak or the Western States 100 are less convenient in this respect, because you may have to wait a year or more for another chance if you go off schedule.

Though races like marathons make superb goals for most runners to use in planning their training, there are a host of noncompetitive objectives that can serve as well. The beginner usually sets intermediate goals as a matter of course. The idea of running around a particular loop or covering a specified distance becomes the focal point of the novice's running for a time, and there is a real sense of achievement when a particular barrier is first passed. With one very steep mountain trail I used for training at one time, my goal was simply to run the entire trail without rest stops or walking breaks, and I was elated the first time I made it. Most runners have had similar experiences.

Such ideas can form the basis of goals for more advanced runners as well. You can work toward the goal of running between two towns, over a particular mountain range, or around a track for a distance of a hundred miles. You may want to do a particular run because it has special aesthetic appeal, because it presents an exciting challenge, or because of an historical race that was run there. Any run that excites your imagination can serve as a worthwhile training goal. Some such runs may require a number of days to complete or consist of a series of routes that have a particular unity.

Unless you have been running a long time, you should try to

pick a goal that you can accomplish during the coming year. Otherwise it is likely to fade too far into the future to provide you with much motivation. Some runners with particularly ambitious designs have set intermediate objectives that serve as stepping stones to their grandiose visions. But it is important that your target is not so far from your grasp that the steps needed to achieve it can't even be worked out. If a particular objective is to serve as a focal point of training, the steps and timetable required to reach it have to be calculable.

DOING THE PAPERWORK

It is easy to decide that you'd like to do something—run over the crest of the Sierra Nevada or finish the Boston Marathon in under three hours. What turns such an idea from a vague aspiration into a realistic motivating force is a specific program to get you there from where you are now. Quite a few chapters in this book are devoted to specific aspects of training that can be included in such a plan, but it might be helpful to consider an example.

Suppose that you have run a previous marathon in three hours and forty-five minutes. You did it last year on a training schedule of seventy miles or so a week. Since then you've continued running, but you've had a few slips in training during vacations and busy periods, and you're currently running thirty miles a week at about eight-minute miles. It's September, and you'd like to run Boston in under three hours next year.

The first step in putting foundations under your dream is to work out a vague timetable. Start off with a set of optimistic estimates, just to see whether the idea makes any sense at all. To continue with the assumptions, we'll make you a male under the age of forty. This means you need to run a three-hour marathon before Boston to qualify officially to run.* If you're going to be reasonable, you'll have to run your three-hour marathon well before Boston to give yourself time for recovery and for

---

*A new qualifying standard of 2:50 was established for 1980.

sending in your application, but let's be generous at the moment and allow only two months before Boston for the qualifying run. Boston takes place in mid-April, so you have to be ready for a three-hour marathon by mid-February. If you live in the northern part of the country, you'll also need to travel to your race. Marathons aren't generally run in the colder states in February, and they wouldn't provide a very reliable chance to qualify for Boston even if they were. Running a three-hour marathon in ice and snow isn't the easiest way to Hopkinton.

Now that you have your three-hour objective backed up to February, let's see how you get there. For a three-hour pace, you will probably want to put in more than your previous seventy miles a week, but a bare minimum would be to do base training at that level for a couple of months, followed by a month of sharpening and speed work. That brings you back to mid-November, at which time you already need to be running seventy miles a week. Before then, you have to move from your current thirty miles a week to seventy. It is generally a bad idea to try to increase mileage any faster than 10 percent each week, so it will take you at least nine weeks to reach seventy miles a week. This very optimistic schedule will barely give you the required training time, yet you are also trying to shave forty-five minutes from your previous marathon time—nearly two minutes per mile faster. It should be obvious that you won't be able to be ready soon enough. A more realistic objective is required, saving Boston for the following year. Running a three-hour marathon at about the time of Boston would probably be a suitable goal, but not doing a qualifying race in February.

The assumptions used in these calculations are discussed thoroughly in the next few chapters, but there are a few important points that should be summarized here. To begin with, the basic training schedule for most serious racers should revolve around a long period of base training: Distance running at moderate levels of stress, designed to build up the runner's stamina, strength, and resistance to injury. The serious racer then prepares for a racing season or a particularly important race by intensive sharpening training designed to bring on peak performance. At the end of the sharpening period, the runner will be able to achieve consistently superior racing times for a period of a month or two, but then has to slack off somewhat and return to base training.

The reason for this cycle is twofold. Racing at your maximum potential and sharpening for it are very hard on the body. Unlike base training, they do not improve your overall well-being or health. On the contrary, if continued too long, they are likely to result in injury or illness, because to reach peak condition, you have to draw a good deal on your body's underlying reserves of strength. The second reason for deliberately peaking has been alluded to before: It is better to deliberately time your peaks for the races in which you want to do best. Nothing is more frustrating than to do well in a series of local fun races and then very poorly in the big race you have been shooting for all year. Not all the greatest stars follow the schedule just described, but there are strong arguments for it, which will be elaborated in later chapters.

There are some important qualifications to this training pattern that should be summarized here. The first is that you should avoid peaking training if you are an average runner and racer and still far from being in good racing form. You can race on base training alone, and providing you keep a reasonable proportion between your training runs and races, you will be able to race fairly well and stay healthy. The purpose of sharpening is precisely to bring on peak performance, and it should not be used lightly or by runners who are not fit enough. Furthermore, it makes no sense to go out and run a hard six weeks of interval training to reduce your time for each mile by ten seconds when you could cut it by twenty seconds by losing a few pounds of excess weight. The runner should be racing fit before doing heavy speed training or other running designed to bring on a peak. Average runners can also use a less intensive peaking regimen that will bring on a more modest improvement in performance at less physical cost, techniques discussed more thoroughly in Chapter X.

Several other major assumptions are made in the calculations above. One is that mileage should not be increased more than 10 percent each week. There are exceptions to this rule, considered in Chapter VI, but usually an average rise of 10 percent should be considered an absolute maximum. That is, you may increase 20 percent one week and hold that mileage figure for several weeks, but planning steady increases in excess of 10 percent will probably cause you to get hurt. Even if you get away with bigger increases, there usually won't be a major gain in training; you will simply spend some time after the big push slogging along and consolidating your gains rather than making new ones. Furthermore, you shouldn't try to increase mileage even this much if you are running faster or introducing new stresses like hill training.

Finally, to calculate the basc mileage needed to run a marathon, there is the formula devised by Ken Young. Young says that assuming ideal conditions, proper pacing, and the like, you can expect to hit the wall and slow radically when you have run one twentieth of your total mileage during the longest consecutive sixty days of recent training. Thus, to run a marathon at something approaching your capacity without hitting the wall you must have run an average of over sixty miles a week for the two months preceding your tapering off for the race. This formula is discussed in more detail in Chapter VI, but it is generally quite reliable, and is the basis for the assumption in the discussion above that you need to plan to run a steady seventy miles a week for a couple of months prior to peaking for a fast marathon.

RACING FOR FUN

Most dedicated runners sooner or later do at least some racing, perhaps because the competitive challenge appeals to them, because they enjoy the social occasion, out of natural curiosity about how well they will perform, or for other related reasons. Since motivations for racing vary so much, the styles of training that are appropriate do also. If you simply run a five-

or ten-mile race every week as your fast training run, taking advantage of a pleasant occasion to get out with friends, there may be no special training involved at all. On the other hand, if you run all of your races hard, you may have to be careful about scheduling them.

Whether they are paced at an effort that is hard or easy, races should be enjoyable. There is a special challenge to racing that makes it different from other kinds of running, and one of the attractions is that racing helps you to run your best. In the artificially controlled situation that they present, races also give you an objective yardstick with which to measure your conditioning. This reason alone often makes occasional racing worthwhile for any dedicated runner. If you run a marathon every twelve months, for example, you can compare the results of your training from one year to the next.

Racing has a number of other attractions, though. Running is usually a solitary sport or one shared with just a few companions. Most of us find this situation to be ideal on a day-to-day basis, but it is also pleasant to meet other runners before and after a race, often including friends with whom you can't train because your schedules are incompatible or because they are much slower or much faster than you are. Racing gives you a chance both to pace yourself against others of roughly your own level of ability and to watch much better runners. One of the virtues of distance running compared with other competitive sports, in fact, is that rank amateurs occasionally have the opportunity to race against some of the world's best athletes. There is a democratic flavor to distance running that is impossible in most sports. The competition is particularly strong in many parts of the United States, because the standards are now so high here. There are literally hundreds of distance runners who would be guaranteed Olympic berths in most countries, but are far from the top rank in the States. The boom in distance running here has occurred at all levels, and there is an amazing number of very-high-standard runners.

After the start, of course, most of us will see only the backs of the best racers, but competition and pacing help from other runners at your own level is a great help in running a good race. Hardly anyone can run as fast in training as he can in a race. As a result, racing teaches you a lot about your own capabilities and allows you to do better in training as well. Racing acts as both a catalyst and a gauge of performance.

There are attractions to particular races that give them special allure. The Boston Marathon is steeped in tradition and in tales of agony and glory. Both Boston and New York have the special excitement generated by crowds of spectators and by the possibility of running a route that is not available at any other time of the year. The Bay to Breakers in San Francisco is almost more of a runner's rite than it is a race. In a well organized race these days a field of several thousand is commonplace. Running in a large group is a stimulating experience, though most of us would not choose it as a steady diet.

There are a few negative aspects associated with the stimulation of racing, however. The adrenaline rush and the thrill of competition that help you to run well are a good thing only if you are in shape for a fast, hard run at the race distance. The attractions of racing derive from its "special" nature, and it is usually a mistake to enter a race with the idea that you will just jog the course. One common self-delusion of a person who is overtraining is to enter a race, do badly, and then convince himself or herself that it was "just a training run." Using low-key races as fast training runs can be fine for experienced runners in reasonably good shape, who can actually run the race at 90-percent effort and finish feeling that it was a good workout. Many runners, though, enter such races when they should be doing base training at a moderate level of effort, yet they're so naturally competitive that they run as hard as possible, usually for much too long a distance. A quick ten-mile race may be just the thing if you have been regularly running eighty or a hundred miles a week for months, but it is a serious race for a person who has been doing forty.

In order to have fun racing, you need to gauge yourself well and avoid entering races that don't fit well into your schedule. The rule of thumb is to train ten miles for every mile raced. This is the distance you should run before the next race, not a cumulative figure. In other words, you should run a hundred training miles following a ten-mile competition before taking on another race. Don't race when you are building up your training stress, whether you are increasing mileage, starting hill work, or introducing stiff *fartlek*. The question of what *really* constitutes racing is relevant, of course. If you run at a relaxed pace in a ten-mile fun run, it doesn't put any more stress on your body than running the same distance alone. You have to keep your judgment clear of wishful thinking, however. Were you really relaxed, or just slow?

The main point of racing for most of us is to add spice to our running. If you race intelligently, you'll enjoy the experience and improve the rest of your running. But too much of an obsession with racing and with racing performances is likely to lead to overtraining and injury. Racing is a little like good wine—don't let it go to your head.

OTHER CHALLENGES

There are lots of other changes of pace that can make running more enjoyable and more interesting. Broadening your experience is usually beneficial to all aspects of your running, as long as it doesn't interfere with important training goals. Taking up mountain running will strengthen the flatlander's legs and ankles. It may cut down your leg speed for a little while, but in the long run it will lead to better times on the flats. For inveterate trail runners, however, an occasional session on the track may turn out to be less boring than anticipated. The controlled situation, uniform surface, and the possibility of concentrating on leg speed and pacing have attractions of their own.

My main argument here, though, is that you should get off your standard running circuits from time to time and use your running as a sort of holiday. Sometimes this may involve an ambitious and grandiose project, like running from one rim of the Grand Canyon to the other or making a running ascent of a high peak. Most of the time, though, it means finding challenging or intriguing runs near home. For your long run of the week, try catching a ride or taking a bus out to another town and running home. Or leave early in the morning so that you can run to a beach or mountain picnic ground where you plan on spending the day with your family.

In the area where I live there are hundreds of possible trail runs within a reasonable distance of my home, as well as canyon roads that make good runs very early in the morning. The possibilities are different in other parts of the country, but there is always some special running route waiting to be found. It may be a twenty mile run along an irrigation ditch, a circuit following the roads around a lake, a trip down the length of a stretch of beach, or an interesting route between two towns. A few detailed local maps will nearly always suggest possibilities. One nice feature of this sort of running is that the better your condition, the more possibilities open up. When you can run only five miles on rough trails, you may be limited to jaunts in the foothills. As twenty- or thirty-mile runs become feasible, you can start thinking about running across mountain ranges.

SOME NOTES FOR WOMEN

There are few sections in this book directed specifically to female runners. This is true mainly because it is addressed to experienced distance runners. There are some significant differences between both the physical and psychological difficulties faced by novice women runners and those faced by neophyte men, as well as differences in the practical trivia of clothing, dealing with chafing, and so forth. But dedicated runners of both sexes have already worked through these beginners' problems. Among serious runners, except at levels of top national and international competition, there are more differences between individual runners than there are between male and female runners as such.

In terms of competition and training for the best runners,

there are still some serious battles to be won. Programs and opportunities for girls and women in schools and collegiate competition are still inferior to those available to their male counterparts. The distance limitations imposed by the American Athletic Union and the International Olympic Committee are so ludicrous that they could not be defended by an intelligent human being without blushing. It is absurd that there are so few top-level long-distance competitions for women within the normal framework of international athletics. This is a political problem that needs serious work.

For most women runners, however, these problems are more an issue of principle (and an important one!) than of practical import. In the United States, distance noninvitational racing events that are generally open to all runners are now open equally to both sexes. In addition, several excellent series of women's races have begun in the last few years.

On questions of training, there is no longer any doubt that women are as capable of running both long and extreme distances as men are, perhaps more so. Average speed is a little slower for women, but the recommendations in this book are formulated so that they can be used by runners of various speeds.

It remains an open question whether female distance runners are really slower than men by nature, or whether this is simply a function of experience, training, and psychological barriers. It is a commonly accepted scientific finding (which may or may not be true) that the differing body composition of women and men makes it impossible for women to be as fast as men in short runs. But even if one accepts the assertion that women will never be able to run the hundred-yard dash as fast as men, it does not follow that the same is true of the 10,000-meter race, the marathon, or 100 miles. Various physiological barriers have been cited to demonstrate such a proposition, but the fact is that we do not really know the limiting parameters of performance even in males, who have been studied far more and who have competed at these distances for a longer time than female athletes.

One can argue that women's generally lower maximum oxygen uptake will prevent their competing on an equal basis in, say, the marathon. But one can argue equally well that the current women's record (2:27:33 at the time this is written, set by Grete Waitz in the 1979 New York race) would have been good enough to win any of the men's Olympic marathons from 1896 to 1952, even though most of these were run over shorter distances than the current standard. Women do have the advantage of starting with current training techniques, and there are many women runners compared to the number of men who used to run long distances. On the other hand, there are still far fewer women running than men, and many of them started at advanced enough ages so that they will never reach their maximum potential. The lack of internationally sanctioned races obviously limits the highest-level performances. Perhaps most important, records are psychological barriers as much as they are physical ones. The four-minute mile, once an "impossible" barrier, became almost commonplace once Roger Bannister had run one. The women's marathon record has continued to decrease at a phenomenal rate. It is not likely that a woman will run a 2:20 next year, but I do expect to see that fairly soon. And who knows where the record will go from there?

The most exciting thing about women's running is that no one really has any idea what the limits are. They will be explored by the current generation of women runners.

CHAPTER IV

BASIC TRAINING PRINCIPLES

MOST DEDICATED RUNNERS are familiar with the basic principles of training, but it is worth reviewing them here as a basis for discussion of more problematic ideas. Training, whether you like to call it that or not, is the only way to improve in running or in any other sport. There are several aspects to training: physical conditioning, the development of reflexes and skills, and the learning of tactics and strategy. In running, of course, physical conditioning is paramount. Methods of relaxing muscles during the final spring after a long run, evolving a slightly more efficient style, or finding effective racing tactics can be important, but only if you are competing with runners in similar condition. A wily old tennis player can beat someone in much better physical shape through superior skill and tactics, but this is true only to a very limited degree in running. You can't use clever tricks on someone who is already three miles ahead of you.

The fundamental principle of training is usually expressed in the language of Hans Selye's theory of stress and adaptation.

By stressing our bodies beyond the level that is easy or comfortable, we stimulate them to adapt to dealing with higher levels of stress. If a particular muscle does very little work it will gradually atrophy, losing both strength and endurance. When it is exercised, the muscle is stimulated to gain in strength and endurance, becoming stronger and able to do still more work. Selye's theory holds that an organism becomes better able to withstand stress through experiencing it, a theory borne out perfectly in the experience of runners. You don't develop the ability to run a marathon or a fifty-miler by sitting at home resting.

SPECIFICITY

One important principle of training is often obscured by our tendency to think in general terms like "good condition," "strength," and "endurance." These expressions have perfectly good meanings, or course, but they sometimes cause us to gloss over the precise goals and effects of our training. The principle of specificity simply holds that training will stimulate the body to adapt to perform in the same way more efficiently. The muscles work best when stressed at a lower level than their maximum capacity; so by working them near that maximum, we stimulate them to become more efficient by increasing their capacities. They improve only in the direction they are pushed, however. Obviously lifting weights with your arms will not strengthen your legs. Moreover, lifting a relatively light weight repeatedly will not enable you to lift a heavier weight, nor will training to lift the heaviest possible weight greatly improve your ability to lift the light one many times. Specificity applies not only to particular muscles but to particular kinds of exercise.

The most obvious consequences of the principle of specificity are easy for the modern runner to apply. Push-ups and pull-ups are fine for overall conditioning and for improving your ability in some other sports, but they will not significantly help your marathoning. (See Chapter VIII for some qualifications of this statement.) Endurance events like twenty-mile road races require distance training for the legs, not just hundred-yard sprints. One of the advances made in training for the distance races during the last few decades has been the development of schedules more specific to the particular events. Most marathoners used to train like middle-distance runners. The debacles that often occurred toward the ends of the races are not surprising; the participants often simply didn't have sufficient endurance training, so that they were forced to flog their bodies to the limit in the later stages of a race.

At more sophisticated levels, however, the principle of specificity becomes far more slippery. The body cannot be pushed to its limits too often, especially in endurance events, so how is one to train for an all-out race? If you want to train for a fifty-mile event, the limits of time alone would likely make it impossible to train by going out to run fifty miles very often. To perform at your best in distance races, you need both endurance and speed, yet trying to combine these in training would turn it into racing instead—so should you train for endurance or for speed? Questions like these are really at the heart of the arguments over different training methods, and they will be the subjects of several subsequent chapters.

STRESS AND RECOVERY

Another clear training principle is that the body can recoup and build its strength only during a period of rest following the hard training session that stimulates it to adapt. Everyone understands this, at least in part, yet it is probably the most widely violated of the really important training principles. Many runners have been crippled by a natural tendency toward impatience, exacerbated by the old macho coaching styles holding that the athlete should "run through the pain" and that training "is no good unless it hurts." Many other runners have never reached their potential because they have paid attention only to the stressful phase of the training cycle and ignored the recovery phase. The single most crucial point about training, though, is that the active improvement phase for your *body* is the recovery phase. You don't become stronger during your exhausting training run; you break down muscle tissue, draw on your reserves, and become weaker. It is during the subsequent period of relaxation that you become stronger. If you cut that period short, the training will have a negative rather than a positive effect.

Of course, the principle of stress and recovery, like that of specificity, is full of subtleties in its application. The length of the recovery period needed is difficult to judge, and there are many kinds of recovery and stress. If you are training for a hundred-mile mountain race, you obviously have to extend the periods of stress so that your body will adapt to making extended efforts. The mixture and operation of various cycles of adaptation and recovery are extremely complex and do not lend themselves well to pat formulae.

But it's not because of the subtleties that most people run into difficulties with the recovery principle. Impatience, self-delusion, and a curious belief that the need for a recovery period applies to everyone but ourselves are the usual reasons for running afoul of this rule. "In pride, in reas'ning pride, our error lies." There is no doubt that the great majority of injuries, along with many uneven performances and frustrating failures to improve, stem from overtraining.

Recovery periods of various sorts will be discussed in later chapters, but Bill Bowerman's basic hard day/easy day routine is the rule of thumb that runners should use to gauge their schedules. Recovery times vary, both between runners and for individuals at different times and phases of training; but it usually requires more than a day to fully recover from a hard training session. Running every day is fine, but don't try to run hard every day. Make sure you take at least one easy recovery day after any hard workout.

AEROBIC AND ANAEROBIC WORK

Most regular runners know the difference between aerobic and anaerobic exercise and training. You are running aerobically when you can maintain a steady pace with regular breathing. You will breathe harder when running aerobically than when you are sitting in a chair reading a book, but you won't start panting or lose your breath. In this kind of running, oxygen is supplied to the muscles at the same rate at which it is burned, and the exercise can be continued at the same pace for a considerable period of time. The chemical reactions that take place in the muscles to oxidize fuel and generate energy are relatively efficient and produce few waste products. The muscles of the body will perform work aerobically when possible, because it is the most efficient way to do work.

When demands are made on the muscles that exceed their ability to produce energy through the aerobic pathway, another method for burning fuel also exists, which allows for brief bursts of speed or strength. It is called anaerobic (without air) because oxygen is not required to do work. Anaerobic exercise can take place even if you are unable to supply oxygen fast enough to produce the necessary energy. Large amounts of energy can be produced quickly through the anaerobic pathway, but the process uses fuel far less efficiently than the aerobic one, and waste products are produced that will cause a rapid collapse from fatigue if they are allowed to build up very long. Almost twenty times as much energy can be produced from muscle glycogen (the sugarlike substance stored in the muscles for fuel) aerobically as anaerobically. Anaerobic exercise also produces lactic acid as a waste product. This lactic acid later has to be oxidized and removed from the muscles when the athlete returns to an aerobic state, and the process requires extra oxygen in addition to the demands of the muscles that are still working.

Moving into an anaerobic state thus produces an "oxygen debt" that the runner has to pay back later, with high interest. It is like a short-term loan; it can be useful to see you through a brief crunch, but if you try to get by on it for a very long period, the interest on the debt soon becomes crushing. A hundred-yard dash can be run almost completely anaerobically because you can pay back the debt at your leisure by collapsing on the grass beyond the finish line. In a long race, however, you should use the anaerobic mechanism very sparingly. A distance racer frequently goes into oxygen debt while pushing up a hill or forcing the pace, but the time soon comes to pay the piper.

Exercise is never purely aerobic or wholly anaerobic. Lactic acid builds up on the most relaxed training runs, and some aerobic work is done even in the shortest sprints. One of the keys to training for maximum performance, in fact, is to increase the speed at which you can run aerobically. It is a major attraction of distance running that this is a form of training that can produce dramatic results, in contrast to basic anaerobic speed, much of which is genetically determined.

Both aerobic and anaerobic training are a part of every well-balanced routine aimed at improving performance, however. Anaerobic training is closely related to the various forms of speed training, because when you try to run very fast, you naturally move into an anaerobic state. Training at levels that push a little beyond your aerobic capacity is also necessary to increase that capacity, as well as to train the legs to move efficiently at a fast pace. There is great disagreement over the proper mixture of aerobic and anaerobic training, however, and this is another subject for later chapters.

LUNGS, HEART, AND CIRCULATION

Before discussing the effects of conditioning on the respiratory and circulatory systems, it is helpful to review how they function together. The blood supplies the tissues of the body with all sorts of necessary substances, but the most immediate needs of the working muscles are to have oxygen delivered and carbon dioxide removed. The carbon dioxide is the product of efficient burning of fuel by the muscles. The muscle cells extract energy by oxidizing the fuel—breaking it down and combining it with oxygen. Oxygen is carried to the muscles by the hemoglobin in the red blood cells.

When you inhale, the fresh air is drawn into tiny passages in the lungs. Both the air passages and the blood vessels in the lungs are divided into vast networks of very fine pathways, separated by the thinnest membranes, so that there is a huge surface area over which the blood and air come into near contact and across which the molecules of carbon dioxide and oxygen can pass. The high concentration of carbon dioxide in the blood that has just returned from the body causes the carbon dioxide to disperse into the freshly inhaled air, which has a low concentration of the gas. Oxygen passes in the opposite direction and is bound by the hemoglobin, which has a high affinity for oxygen.

The heart is divided into two sides. The right side of the heart receives the oxygen-poor blood from the veins of the body and pumps it through the lungs and back to the left side of the heart. The left side then pumps the oxygenated blood through the main arteries of the body to the working muscles and the other organs and tissues.

Oxygenated blood passes first through large arteries which then separate again and again into smaller branches. Blood vessels supplying a working muscle finally split into microscopic channels called capillaries, with walls made up of a single layer of sheathing cells. It is in the network of capillaries known as the capillary bed that oxygen and nutrients are extracted from the blood by the working cells, to be replaced by carbon dioxide and waste products. The blood is then gathered again through a network of progressively larger veins and returned to the right side of the heart.

As most experienced runners these days know, fitness of the respiratory and circulatory systems is the most fundamental form of conditioning, especially for distance work. One of the main reasons for the current popularity of running is that it is such an effective way of improving the efficiency of the lungs, heart, and the circulatory system. Cardiopulmonary fitness carries over into many other kinds of activity, giving a good capacity for hard work over long periods of time.

As with nearly all the working parts of the body, the cardiopulmonary system operates most efficiently when it is functioning well below maximum capacity. Thus, if two people with exactly the same body build and style are running at an identical pace, but one is using 80 percent of his or her maximum capacity to transport oxygen, while the other is using only 60 percent, the first runner will not only be closer to the limit but will actually be using more energy as well. Training to increase cardiopulmonary fitness thus both improves the maximum working level of the body and increases its efficiency at lower levels of effort.

For the beginner and for many runners at intermediate levels, cardiopulmonary fitness is the major limiting factor in long-distance capacities. Such people can run fast, but they can't run fast for long periods without losing their breath. The limitations of anyone's capacity to run involve complex relationships among a number of factors; but it is clear that for those who are not highly trained, the most important limitation is the inability to deliver sufficient oxygen to the working muscles. Any attempts to run at high speed require a heavy reliance on anaerobic energy sources, so that the runner is soon gasping for breath and fatigued from lactic acid buildup.

It is interesting to note that this is not true for very highly trained runners, at least not in nearly so direct a way. They find it far easier to keep their muscles supplied with oxygen. One demonstration of this fact is the performance of athletes who live and train at high altitudes compared with that of sea-level athletes. The high-altitude individuals develop a better capacity to transport oxygen by training in air that has less of it, and they have a definite advantage in races that are held at high elevations, where the sea-level runners cannot supply adequate oxygen to their muscles. In contrast, however, this extra capacity gives no advantage to high-altitude athletes in a race held at sea level, where other limiting factors dominate.

The development of cardiopulmonary fitness is a slow process, one that takes place through long-term training. It develops more quickly than factors such as joint strength, but not nearly so quickly as leg speed. One of the purposes of extended base training is thus to improve cardiopulmonary effectiveness.

A number of improvements occur as the runner becomes more fit. The increased stroke volume of the heart is an aspect that has received much attention. The heart pumps more blood with each stroke, so that it does not have to beat as rapidly to transport the same amount of blood through the lungs and body. This is the reason why most people's resting pulse gradually becomes slower as they attain greater fitness. Pulse rate is not an accurate index of fitness, but its decline is a very common indication that the runner is becoming better conditioned. Very low resting pulse rates are commonplace among trained runners. (An accurate indication of a high level of conditioning is the rapidity with which the pulse returns to normal after heavy exercise.)

A more important consequence of increased stroke volume is that because the heart rate is high, the heart can pump much more blood than it could with a lower stroke volume. Since maximum heart rate is independent of training, this is the mechanism by which the body is able to deliver more blood, and thus more oxygen, to the muscles. The maximum heart rate declines inexorably with age, but the pumping capacity of the heart in a highly trained middle-aged runner may exceed that of the average young man or woman because of increased stroke volume.

The mechanical aspect of the respiratory cycle—moving air in and out of the lungs—becomes more efficient in several ways. The most important of these is the training effect in the breathing muscles, which have to be conditioned for hard endurance work like any other muscles of the body. This is particularly true since the chest expands and contracts farther during hard breathing than it does during relaxed respiration, while working faster at the same time. When you are at rest or doing only light work, for example, no effort at all is involved in exhalation. Your diaphragm contracts to expand the chest cavity and inflate the lungs, but expiration of the air is accomplished by simply relaxing the muscle and allowing the chest to contract. During hard breathing, considerable effort is used during both inhalation and exhalation.

The maximum amount of air you can exhale after breathing in as deeply as possible is called your vital capacity. There is some disagreement among the authorities over whether or not training by adults increases vital capacity. There is no question, however, that conditioning does enable you to move more air through your lungs during a given period of time. Increased muscular efficiency is probably the main factor, though lowered resistance to the movement of air through the lungs and increased vital capacity may also be factors. The increase in the quantity of air that can be processed is about 25 percent, which is a very significant rise, even without the usual reduction in body weight associated with training.

Long-term participation in endurance training also stimulates changes in the ability of the muscles involved to take up and use oxygen. The capillary bed of the muscle becomes better developed. There are also chemical changes at the cellular level that result in more efficient oxygen uptake.

The combined effects of all these changes result in the trained athlete's being able to use far more oxygen than an untrained individual can. This increased ability to process oxygen is certainly the greatest single factor in initial phases of training, particularly if it is considered in proportion to body weight. The capacity to use a large quantity of oxygen per unit of body weight is a precondition to good running performance. It is probably the best measure of cardiopulmonary fitness.

The maximum uptake of oxygen per unit time for each pound of a runner's body weight is measured during a run at the highest level of effort. One does not find, however, that the best runners have the highest uptake, only that a high uptake is characteristic of all good runners. Other factors, such as efficiency of the use of oxygen and the ability to sustain a very high proportion of maximum uptake for long periods, seem more important than top capacity. This finding compares with the failure of high-altitude-trained runners to outperform those from low altitude. Both results imply that the oxygen uptake is not the limiting factor for top runners.

HOW THE BODY MOVES

There are several types of muscle in the body. The heart muscle, for example, is highly specialized and quite different from the muscles in the arms or legs. The heart, the diaphragm, and other specialized muscles involved in the vital functions of the body are related to running in a supportive role. Those muscles specifically used to move the runner, however, are all skeletal muscles. Each one is normally attached to two bones, either directly or with an inelastic fibrous band called a tendon.

The basic framework of the body is made up of bones. They are living and active tissue just as organs and muscles are, but they are fairly rigid in adults. The bones meet in joints, which are shaped depending on their specific functions. Some joints are almost completely immobile in adulthood, like those in the skull, while others allow a great deal of motion between the bones. The joints are bound with fibrous bands called ligaments. (Ligaments and tendons are similar, but a ligament binds two bones together, while a tendon joins a muscle to a bone.)

The joints also have a variety of special slippery tissues: sacs filled with fluid, slippery cushioning pads, and secretors of liquid to provide lubrication, all serving to facilitate motion. Naturally, those joints that bear the weight of the body require more elaborate structures to prevent grating and damage during motion. The weight-bearing joints vary a good deal in structure. The hip joint, which is designed to permit a wide range of motion in any direction, is a ball-and-socket joint. The knee, which is the largest joint in the body, consists of two ball-and-socket joints side by side, so that motion is limited to a single plane. The ankle joint is a saddle which the two bones of the lower leg straddle like a rider on a horse.

The skeletal muscles serve to move the bony framework and also to hold it together. There are muscular structures around all the active joints which stabilize them and hold them in place, and during normal motion the strength of the ligaments is not tested. They serve primarily in a reserve capacity to prevent excessive joint motion when the capacity of the muscles is exceeded because of fatigue or accident.

Skeletal muscles are normally attached to the bones on either side of a joint so that they can exert force on both bones and pull them closer together. Muscles cannot exert force in lengthening; they can only contract and pull in tension or relax and become passive. Motion in the opposite direction has to be initiated by another muscle or by an external force like gravity. Thus, skeletal muscles are always paired off with antagonistic muscles that pull in the opposite direction. There are normally many muscles arranged in an array around a joint to stabilize it and to produce the motions of the bones that meet at the joint. Around an important joint that has freedom to move in many directions like the hip joint there have to be dozens of muscles to hold the joint in place and to move the bones in every desired direction. Most muscles are attached to bones on either side of a single joint, while others cross two different joints.

When you move any part of your body a complicated series of action has to be coordinated by the nervous system. The muscles on one side of a joint have to contract at the required speed and with enough force to overcome resistance, other muscles have to relax so that they do not oppose the motion, and still others may be needed to provide tension to stabilize a joint throughout the motion. Efficient neural direction of all these actions in exactly the right order is a crucial component of efficient movement, and this kind of coordination is one of the factors that improves with training. An important function of speed work in the training schedules of racers is the development of efficient movement at racing speed. Slight defects in timing of the relaxation of opposing muscles or imperfectly synchronized signals to the contracting muscles will reduce speed and waste energy.

MUSCLE STRUCTURE AND COMPOSITION

The cells of skeletal muscles consist of fibers arranged in bundles that are set in motion by a single nerve. The nerve has multiple endings to activate the individual muscle cells. One nerve is thus likely to direct over a hundred individual muscle fibers. The entire group is known as a *motor unit.* Because fibers in the motor unit are stimulated to contract by different branches of the same nerve, they cannot be activated separately.

When a muscle contracts to perform work, not all of the muscle fibers or motor units are used. Some motor units are recruited, while others remain passive rather than performing work during the contraction. To do relatively light work, such as lifting a pencil, only a few motor units have to be recruited. To pick up a heavy barbell, many motor units have to be activated at the same time. After active contraction, an individual fiber needs time to recuperate before being used again, so heavy work that requires the recruitment of a large number of motor units cannot be repeated often without exhausting the muscle.

Within a skeletal muscle there are fibers of more than one type, though all the fibers in a particular motor unit are normally the same. The most common classification of fibers is into white and red fibers, or fast- and slow-twitch fibers. There are some important qualifications, which will be dealt with in a moment, but white fibers are normally considered the fast-twitch type and red fibers the slow-twitch type. Fast-twitch fibers, as the name implies, reach peak tension much more quickly than slow-twitch ones; they contract more than twice as fast. Slow-twitch muscle fibers, on the other hand, tend to have a better blood supply and to be better able to use fuel aerobically, so that they are superior for endurance exercise.

It has been found that the leg muscles of sprinters have a higher percentage of fast-twitch fibers than average, while those of long-distance runners have a higher percentage of slow-twitch fibers than the norm. This makes sense from what we know about the demands of these two types of exercise and the characteristics of the fibers. Slow-twitch red fibers, with their superior capacity to oxidize fuel and to do work over long periods, clearly are better suited for extended efforts, while the fast-twitch white fibers provide the amazing power and speed of the sprinter. It has generally been assumed that the distribution of fiber types is inherited and that the capacity for long-, middle-, or short-distance running is therefore largely determined genetically by the proportion of the types of fibers in the leg muscles. There are some major complications with this idea, however.

To begin with, there are really a number of ways to classify muscle fibers, and the labeling of a particular fiber can differ depending on what the observer looks for. There seems to be some gradation in the function and operation of the cells that does not fall into nearly as neat a pattern as the fast white/slow red division suggests. Cells normally labeled white actually can be divided into at least two distinct types, one having a higher aerobic potential than the other. All muscle fibers are able to function both aerobically and anaerobically, and they can also be significantly modified by training. The fast-twitch fibers in particular improve their capacity for oxidizing fuel very significantly as a result of endurance training.

Furthermore, there is strong evidence to suggest that fiber types may change as a result of training, so that theories based on genetic determination of fiber distribution may be altogether wrong. The evidence from research at the moment is unclear on this whole question.

What is known for certain is that much of the long-term training effect that takes place during endurance running occurs at the cellular level. The number of capillaries around each muscle cell increases with extended training, and the enzyme activity in the muscle changes in ways that improve the capacity of aerobic work and reduce the tendency of the cells to burn fuel anaerobically. These cellular changes occur in a different pattern from the improvements in the ability of the lungs and heart to deliver oxygen to the body as a whole. The differing rates of the body in responding to training in the central system and in the muscles constitute one of the factors that make training schedules hard to design and use effectively.

EFFICIENCY AND AEROBIC WORKING LEVEL

The improvement of the runner's capacity for maximum oxygen consumption is important for beginning and intermediate-level runners, but it is not the deciding factor in ability between the best distance runners. Two capacities that are more important are the runner's efficiency level while moving at a particular speed and the degree to which he or she can approach maximum oxygen consumption without relying heavily on anaerobic metabolism. These elements are important for any dedicated runner.

Efficiency is really the end result of a whole complex of training effects, along with natural ability and psychological factors. An efficient runner can move along next to a less efficient one, while burning less fuel and oxygen. Biomechanical structure, running style, neuromuscular coordination, weight, and the ability to concentrate on efficient movement are some of the factors that play a part. These are all affected by training, and the type of training is important. For example, one benefit of training at race pace is that it allows the runner to learn to relax the other muscles of the body while running fast. This reduces energy consumption in other parts of the body, allowing the runner to move efficiently. It is a skill that definitely has to be learned, particularly for the later stages of a long race, when a runner tends to tighten up and move inefficiently just when reserves are limited. Another factor is the ability of the motor units in the muscle to work in unison and the ability of opposing motor units to relax completely, so that each cell contributes to forward motion rather than working against it. This is another important factor in efficiency that develops to an optimum level only through practice at the specific pace, though other factors in efficient movement are best developed in other ways.

The ability to work very close to one's maximum oxygen consumption level is a distinguishing mark in the best distance runners. Top-ranked marathon runners can maintain well over 80 percent of their maximum oxygen consumption rate throughout an entire race. Most runners reaching this level of oxygen consumption would already be using anaerobic metabolism to a considerable degree and would show quite a bit of buildup of lactic acid in short order. The ability to perform for long periods at a high percentage of maximum oxygen consumption is clearly important to the distance runner. There is no doubt that properly planned training increases this ability, so it is an important consideration in planning a training regimen. It may be that the upper limits are defined by genetic factors such as body build and muscular composition. Long-term training effects on this and other characteristics have never been thoroughly studied. It is clear that this type of ability results in part from years of intensive training. It is very difficult, if not impossible, to do controlled experiments on this type of training, so that beyond a certain point, educated guesses have to take over from solid scientific knowledge. (The difficulty arises from the fact that no one dedicated enough to engage in years of hard training is willing to have it dictated by the needs of an experimenter.)

BODY WEIGHT

As most runners know, body weight is a crucial factor in running efficiency. A runner carrying extra weight simply cannot run as far or as fast as someone who is thinner and is otherwise in equivalent condition. There are slight differences in weight that are attributable to bone mass. Muscular build is far more significant, and a person with a heavily muscled upper body will be significantly heavier than someone who is lean and stringy. Except for extreme cases like body builders, however, most weight differences between people of the same sex and height are due almost completely to fat. When the food you eat exceeds what you use, your body stores the surplus in the form of fat deposits. This was a useful evolutionary development for a creature that often had to travel long distances in search of game or plant food, but it is a mixed blessing for residents of modern industrial nations.

For the runner at least, stored fat is a double drag on the body. It has to be moved when you run without making a useful contribution to the body's function. Most of the work that you do in running consists of lifting or accelerating the body's weight, especially that of the legs. Carrying an extra twenty or forty pounds requires a lot of extra work, rather like wearing a suit full of lead weights. Fat is even more demanding than a weight suit, however, because it is living tissue that has to be supplied with oxygen and nutrients, in competition with the working portions of the body. The amount of fat carried by most Americans of "average" build is quite amazing. Most of my friends think I look slim when I am carrying thirty pounds of extra fat, and a taller person would find this true with even more weight.

The influence of weight on running performance is clear enough if you look at a few top long-distance runners. They are uniformly thin, and many would consider them "unhealthy looking." At a more modest standard of performance, a few extra pounds is less critical, but there is no doubt that it is impossible to achieve one's best running potential with any significant amount of fat on the body. The degree to which this is important to individual runners varies widely. If you have very much extra fat, it affects your health as well; but the only thing known for sure about the extra ten pounds or so that separates the person with 5 percent body fat from one with 12 percent is that the lighter person will be able to run faster.

Runners do vary widely in their tendency to put on fat. Those with a naturally lean build never have to worry about very large amounts of fat. For them, being fat is tipping the scales at a few pounds over their weight at top competitive form. Others of us have far more tendency to put on weight, even when we are training. Those who tend to put on fat will send the scale flying when they reduce their mileage over the winter months, when they are injured, or during a period of major work or social demands. There is no question that running is helpful in maintaining a reasonable weight, but individuals vary widely in the degree to which they can simply eat what they want without considering caloric intake. Some suggestions for those who tend to put on weight are included in Chapters XI and XIII.

JOINTS, TENDONS, AND SKELETAL STRUCTURE

It is important for serious runners at all levels of skill to understand that conditioning takes place in the bones, joints, ligaments, and tendons, just as it does in the muscles and the cardiopulmonary system. Bones can become heavier and stronger with conditioning, and so can the other structural supports for the body. They respond to training much more slowly than the muscles and the breathing and circulatory systems, however, and this fact accounts for many of the training injuries suffered by runners.

The difference in the speed of adaptation of the structural elements of the body, particularly in middle-aged and older persons, can be the source of a good deal of frustration to the dedicated runner, because it sets definite limits on the rate at which training can be increased. The syndrome in overenthusiastic runners is as predictable as clockwork: A heavy training schedule increases the runner's aerobic capacity and muscular ability at a rapid rate, and the runner keeps upping the pace and distance until the load exceeds the tolerance level of the tendons, joints, or ligaments. A combination of euphoria and an attitude of invincibility lulls the runner into ignoring the warning signs—the aching tendons or joints, gradually increasing each day—until a really serious injury has developed. The pattern is nearly independent of the actual susceptibility of the runner to injury; running allows you to put sufficient stress on your body to guarantee an eventual breakdown if you push your limits too hard. A muscle pull may intervene first, especially if you do a lot of speed or interval work, but usually the breakdown occurs in the joints, tendons, or ligaments because of their slower rate of adaptation.

You can avoid a good deal of the frustration associated with this syndrome if you realize its causes. The fact that your knees hurt when you raise your training level to seventy-five miles a week does not mean that you will never be able to run that far. It probably means that you have to give your knees time to adapt to the new level of stress. This requires patience—a virtue that many dedicated runners lack, but which has to be acquired if you are to avoid injury. You may find that a defect in foot or leg structure needs correction as well, but orthotic foot supports and the like (see Chapter XIV) are not a panacea either. Shoes or supports can only reduce the shock of footstrike somewhat and balance the stresses within the feet and legs. They may allow you to run a little farther or faster before you break down, and they may shift the weakest zone from one part of your body to another, but they will not prevent you from getting hurt if you train too hard.

The crucial point to remember is that the blood supply and the speed at which the body can repair damage is much poorer in the structural framework of the body than in the muscles and circulatory system. Cartilage and ligaments heal very slowly when they are damaged. Tendons have an extremely poor blood supply. Bones can be healed or strengthened only very slowly. The impatience of a runner who has recently discovered the virtues of training often exceeds the ability of these structures to adapt. If you realize that they will in fact become stronger provided you apply stress *sensibly,* you will be far less likely to suffer serious and lengthy injuries.

SUMMARY

In this chapter I have tried to survey some of the underlying physiological principles that are the basis of any system of training, as a foundation for discussion of the specific techniques that are considered in the following chapters. You should always understand exactly what you are trying to do with particular training methods, whether long, slow distance, hill running, intervals, or any other device. This is equally true for the serious marathoner trying to compete at the world-class level and for the middle-aged runner who is interested primarily in physical conditioning and running for fun. Misconceived methods can cause frustrating results or injuries to both.

The fundamental aspects of base conditioning include weight

reduction for those who do not already have a low body-fat content and conditioning of the respiratory and circulatory systems. The overall improvements in delivery of oxygen to the working muscles come from changes within the skeletal muscles as well as in the heart, respiratory muscles, and other supportive systems. At higher levels of training, the ability to consume a large percentage of maximum oxygen uptake is more of a governing factor for the distance runner than is the absolute value of that maximum. Frank Shorter does not have a particularly high maximum uptake, but he was one of the most consistent winners of world-class distance events for years.

In addition to overall cardiopulmonary fitness and the actual mechanical strength of the skeletal and other supporting structures, various features in the coordination of the contraction of individual motor units, muscle cell types, and a number of other complex factors are influenced by training programs. A good training program should consider all these factors, as well as more specific ones like pacing and acclimatization to heat or altitude.

CHAPTER V

TRAINING METHODS

ANY TRAINING PROGRAM is bound to be made up of many elements, whether it is devised for an Olympic athlete or a middle-aged jogger. The body has ebbs and flows, short- and long-term, and these blend with the cycles of stress and recuperation that are the essence of any conditioning program. A run that is identical in terms of the objective measurements of distance covered and time required will feel easy, relaxed, and exhilarating on one day but difficult, stressful, and tiring the next. On the other hand, few runners design the variations with a conscious plan for getting the best effect from their running.

Before discussing specific schedules, it is useful to define some general training methods, with the understanding that these routines actually blend into one another and are not always as distinctive as their proponents seem to imply. It is also crucial to understand that any adjectives like *fast, slow, hard,* and the like are to be understood relative to the runner and the distance being covered. "Long, slow distance" may mean twenty miles at a seven-minute-per-mile pace for a top-level marathoner or five miles at twelve minutes per mile for a person who has been running for only six months and is still working off the effects of years of inactivity. Even at the level of serious competition, "distance work" and "race tempo" will have quite different meanings for ultramarathoners than for middle-distance runners. It would therefore be impossible to maintain a perfectly uniform training schedule even if it were desirable. We naturally change our routes, distance, pace, and the type of running to conform with all sorts of variables. But few runners put enough thought into planning their training to get the results they want over the long run. Different types of training have different effects on the body, and mixing them at random is no more likely to work well than an arbitrary combination of cooking ingredients. Honey, soy sauce, red wine, and bananas may all be delicious, but not when they are simply tossed together in the pot. By the same token, intervals or hill training may bring out your best when used at the right time. Done at the wrong time they can turn your running stale or leave you unable to run for months. Good training has to be carefully planned.

A lot of confusion can be eliminated as long as one keeps in mind that references have to be relative. "Race pace" for a marathon means five-minute miles to a world-class runner and eight-minute miles to a woman trying to qualify for Boston. During the later sections in the book, where specific recommendations are made, we will attempt to relate training guidelines to those indications that apply equally to *all* experienced runners, regardless of class—heart rates, recovery times, fatigue, and other feedback from the body telling us the effects that training is having.

LONG, SLOW DISTANCE

This term, LSD for short, was coined by Joe Henderson to describe the type of running that is the staple of most serious runners' training schedules these days. The theories behind this style of training have been worked out by a number of runners and coaches, most notably Dr. Ernst van Aaken, Tom Osler, and Henderson. The idea of long, slow distance is to do the bulk of your running at speeds that are enjoyable and that stress your body (mildly) by their duration rather than their intensity. The capacity for aerobic exercise over extended periods is developed, your collapse point is pushed out so that you can run longer and longer without experiencing the radical slowing and leaden limbs that accompany the exhaustion of glycogen reserves. The body learns to use fat as fuel more of the time, so that great stores of muscle glycogen can be held in store for periods of heavy demand. Body weight can be reduced while the heart, the lungs, and the system of oxygen extraction in the muscle cells are slowly improved.

Perhaps most important, the muscles, tendons, bones, ligaments, and joints can strengthen themselves through extended running with relatively low stress. Overuse injuries manifest themselves much more slowly at moderate speed, and it is much easier to correct problems before they become serious. The idea of easy and relaxed running reduces the psychological pressure that runners often impose on themselves. A self-inflicted drive to improve every day is what causes most injuries.

Long, slow distance does not mean jogging the same route every day or plodding along all the time, but it does refer to training with a minimum of top-speed work, anaerobic running, or frequent hangovers from hard training the day before. LSD may be combined with other types of training, but the idea is to spend most of the time at a relatively relaxed speed. That speed will increase gradually for most runners over a long period, but LSD will not bring on rapid improvements.

One disadvantage of LSD is that it can turn you from a runner into a plodder, if you become so obsessed with going slowly that you forget the fun of running. Introducing some kind of speed play occasionally, even during base training periods, avoids staleness and keeps you from settling into a monotonous pace. For top competitors there is the definite disadvantage that LSD does not condition the motor units and neural system for fast running. This disadvantage can be overcome by going through a sharpening phase prior to a serious racing season, but a person training mainly with slow distance will not be able to compete at top form throughout the year. Using LSD does allow the competitor to peak at the desired time, however, and greatly reduces the chances of injury.

Another disadvantage of LSD is that it can degenerate into mileage mania as a substitute for speed mania. LSD will allow you to cover more mileage than speed work. If you push up your mileage beyond your body's tolerance, however, especially if you compulsively insist on piling up the miles when your body is crying for mercy, you will break down just as surely as the speed freak.

Finally, advocates of "quality" over "quantity" argue that LSD is an inefficient way to train. For those with limited time, they argue, 70 miles of properly distributed training will have the same results as 120 slow miles on the roads, and requires a far more reasonable investment of time and energy, one that is much more feasible for many people. Some proponents of this view manage to race at the top level on 70 miles a week. My own feeling is that for most runners, a lot of base mileage at moderate efforts is necessary to build good tolerance for more "quality" training. This seems particularly true for older runners, who can injure themselves very easily by building speed up too fast.

FAST DISTANCE

High mileage, once a rarity, has become commonplace during the last few years. This has resulted from a number of related developments. The immense growth in distance running has resulted in hundreds of thousands of runners doing extended distance work for physical conditioning, personal satisfaction, and race training. Older runners, besides obtaining other benefits from running long distances, have found that this type of training is far better suited to their bodies and temperament than fast intervals on the track. The growing popularity of recreational distance running has also made distance events in serious competition much more popular. These events were once eclipsed by sprints and middle-distance events, but marathons all over the country are now popular spectator sports.

At the same time, serious competitive runners have found that much greater mileage is necessary to do well in competition. Under the influence of coaches like Arthur Lydiard, extended mileage on the roads is the staple of the training of every competitor except the sprinter. Even the middle-distance specialist today is likely to put in more mileage during a year than the marathoner of a few years ago. Among serious runners, including many who are far from the top level of competition, mileages in excess of 100 miles a week are quite common. Most top-level marathoners now run at least that far. Seventy-five miles per week—an average of more than ten miles a day, every day—is now considered to be low mileage for a serious marathoner and commonplace for the average distance runner. Most serious middle-distance runners average at least seventy-five miles a week.

At the same time, with the rising standards in marathon running and the greater prestige of the event, particularly in the United States, many runners who are very fast at shorter distances have worked up to the marathon distance, bringing with them their speed and training methods. A few years ago a 2:30 marathoner was pretty hot stuff; he could have won a good many marathons and placed very well even in the big ones. In 1978, a 2:30 at Boston would only have been good for 162nd place. Much of the reason derives from the fact that there are so many runners, of course; but it is high mileage that enables most of them to compete at such an impressive level.

Many top runners do most of their distance work at fairly high speeds. Their feeling is that training at closer to race pace is far more specific to the needs of the racer, since it builds coordination, efficiency, and endurance for fast running. Advocates of fast distance training consider it to be more productive conditioning, having a greater training effect because a fast run requires less time while stressing the body more than a slower-paced run. Doing a lot of hard, fast mileage can also build great endurance and reserves of strength if the runner does not overstress the body. It allows the racer to compete and turn in a creditable performance at virtually any time during the year rather than slow down during some seasons.

The real disadvantage of fast distance is the risk of overstress to the body, often resulting in serious and frustrating injuries that take a long time to heal. Some runners manage to run hard training sessions regularly for extended periods and apparently thrive on the regimen. Those who stay healthy have learned to judge perfectly the fine line between effective training and overwork. This is a dangerous tactic, however. It is easy to see when others are overtraining, but it is much easier to fool yourself, ignoring warning signs of excessive stress until it is too late. It is characteristic of dedicated runners in good condition that they are able to push themselves and draw on their reserves to a far greater degree than the average person. It is easy to push over the line without noticing. Middle-aged runners who have been at the sport for only a couple of years should be particularly wary of this type of training, since it is very easy to pull a muscle, injure a joint, or create a stress fracture with this type of running unless you have been doing serious training for years—particularly if you lack the fast recuperation times of younger people.

One other disadvantage of fast distance is that it makes planning peaks difficult or impossible. Peaks and valleys often come anyway, but they come at random, usually not when you would wish, leaving you stale for a big race or susceptible to illness in the middle of winter. Most of the top runners who train with fast distance all the time also try to maintain their peak constantly. This is generally a delusion and produces inconsistent performances. If you are tempted to imitate the current superstar in this respect, keep in mind that many earlier practitioners of this style finally crashed. Even if a few runners get away with the tactic, it is rarely successful for long even among the world-class runners. For those of us who are mere mortals, it is almost a guaranteed formula for disaster. (The subject of peaking is discussed in detail in Chapter X.)

Naturally, there is really a continuum of speeds between "fast" and "slow" distance, and a lot of confusion over the prescriptions of some of the great modern coaches is due to ambiguities over the speed and effort that the runner should try to achieve at a particular training level. Much of the emphasis of the slow-distance advocates is on attitude rather than slow speed per se, their point being that the runner should enjoy the training runs and avoid overstress, rather than concentrate on times and pacing as a constant diet. The whole subject of speed, distance, and effort during base training is discussed more extensively in Chapter VI.

INTERVALS

Intervals provide one of the runner's most useful training tools, as well as one of the most maligned, misunderstood, and misused. The principle of interval training is to run a sequence of relatively short distances at a hard pace, alternating them with rests, walks, or slower-paced running. Technically, the resting periods were the ones originally referred to as "intervals," but the common usage is to call the running segments by that name—for example, "Run a dozen 220-yard intervals with 220 jogs in between."

Interval theory was developed by two German scientists during the 1930's. The basic idea is that the body can be trained most quickly and most efficiently by alternating hard work with recuperation periods within a training session, instead of doing continuous exercise to exhaustion, whether at high intensity or low. It has been conclusively proven that an athlete can do far more high-intensity running during a workout if it is done for short periods, interspersed with recuperation intervals, than if the running is continuous. This is because there is much less buildup of lactic acid and other waste products in the muscles when the rest periods are included. You are therefore able to get many of the benefits of speed training with a higher volume of work than would be possible if you simply went out and ran hard until exhaustion set in.

The advantages of interval training are basically those shared by all types of speed work, with the additional benefit of enabling you to do a high volume of training. Speed work allows you to apply a great deal of training stress on the body. Leg speed, coordination of nerves and motor units, and a development of high tolerance for anaerobic exercise are all improved by speed work. You learn to run at race pace and faster, and can develop good pacing judgment and an understanding of your tolerance for putting on bursts of speed and maintaining pace afterward.

Interval training is also more precise than many other running activities, so that it gives the runner an exact notion of what he or she is doing and how it compares with the training load on other days and in other seasons. If you look back in your training diary for last year, an entry that says you did a particular interval routine in certain times is much more informative than a note that you ran ten miles on the roads at "moderate effort." One reason that many coaches like intervals so much is that it gives them exact control over what each runner is doing. Besides, writing out an interval workout looks so scientific!

Interval workouts are also excellent discipline for the racer. It is a lot harder to fake an interval workout, whether you are running against a stopwatch or not, than it is to fake a road run. On the road or trail it is easy to relax and lose your concentration. That is one of the attractions of simply going out for a pleasant run. If you want a hard workout, however, running intervals on a track or some other specified course forces you to be aware of exactly how much effort you are putting into a training session. This is clear whether you are timing yourself or not.

For all these reasons, interval training is one of the best kinds of speed work, especially for sharpening after many months of base training. The runner who is already strong and well conditioned can develop leg speed very quickly and efficiently with a few interval sessions a week. The main disadvantages of interval training are those of any speed work. It can be hard on the legs and can precipitate injuries, especially in runners without an adequate training base. Intervals produce quick results, but they are not a particularly efficient way to build up endurance. The runner can get hurt or go stale quickly, too. Psychologically, it is difficult to avoid a continuous quest for improvement from one session to the next when you are running intervals. Once the inevitable plateau or decline in performance occurs, it can be very discouraging.

Most runners also find intervals boring, particularly as a steady diet. It is a lot easier to persuade yourself to go out for a road or trail run than it is to run 25 × 440 yards, 220 jogs. For this reason, it seems best to save the interval sessions for sharpening before a racing season or an occasion when you want to improve your speed after extensive distance training. Interval training is discussed in more detail in Chapter X.

FARTLEK

Fartlek is a Swedish term, usually translated as "speed play." It is an informal and enjoyable style of interval training in which the pace and length of speed bursts are determined by the runner. It is ideal when you are training with a group of fairly evenly matched runners, especially on the trail runs for which it was originally designed. One runner will initiate a faster interval, perhaps pushing the pace up a hill, running at a relaxed pace for a few hundred yards, and then speeding up to fast tempo for the next rolling half-mile. Depending on how they feel, the other runners may keep up, push to the lead, or fall back for a while. The idea is to gain the benefits of an interval session without its boredom and with a little more attention paid to the dictates of the body. On occasions when you feel strong, you push harder; but when you don't feel quite so well, you run an easier workout. *Fartlek* workouts can be run on the road and alone, as well as with groups and on trails. The advantages of pleasant running with enjoyable and intense pushes interspersed with relaxed motion are obvious, and a good *fartlek* workout can be just as effective as an interval session.

The main disadvantages of *fartlek* compared with intervals also derive from its unstructured character. There is no precision in either distance or time to give the runner an exact feeling for pace or progress. It is easy for the runner to either work too hard or not hard enough, unless progress is occasionally checked by a session on measured courses. These problems are less important to the distance runner who is simply trying to reach peak form for personal satisfaction than they are to the serious competitive athlete who has to reach a certain level in order to race successfully. Even if you are planning to run a race for personal satisfaction, however, some measured running will be important to allow you to pace yourself correctly in the excitement of the start. *Fartlek,* run either alone or with friends, can be used for most sharpening, but it needs to be supplemented with some work on the track or over measured distances on the roads.

A lighter variety of *fartlek* can also be used as a part of base training and is described in the next chapter. Basically, the form is the same, with varied pacing, acceleration, and easy running mixed together according to how you feel. The emphasis during base training, however, is on mixed aerobic running with little pure speed. Such *fartlek* is excellent both for improving your aerobic pace and for experimenting with running style to improve efficiency and reduce the impact of running on your legs. Try working into a gradual acceleration while concentrating on a smooth, effortless style, light footfalls, an upright position with your hips pulled forward, and complete relaxation. Continue the acceleration until you become tense or begin to lose your breath, and then slow down again.

TEMPO TRAINING, PACE WORK, AND TIME TRIALS

The function of interval and *fartlek* training is to improve leg speed and to develop efficiency and relaxation at a fast pace, as well as anaerobic capacity and tolerance for oxygen debt. Intervals are often run at faster than race pace, and their main purpose is to allow the runner to squeeze large quantities of speed work into one session. Longer distances at a fast pace would either require slowing as fatigue built up or impose stresses comparable to those encountered in races. Some training at speed over long distances is also required for good race performances, however. It has to be used sparingly and at the right point in training, as discussed in Chapter X, but it is essential for balanced sharpening and for developing the sense of pace required for effective racing.

There are many terms used to describe longer runs at a fast speed, and their use is often determined more by the runner's immediate objective than by any major differences between them. A time trial is simply a run of a certain distance at race pace, serving both to test the results of sharpening and to harden the runner to the combination of distance and speed. Thus, a marathoner might do a ten-mile time trial a couple of weeks before an important race. It would serve to put a final edge on the racer's condition and to give a precise reading of the correct pace and strategy for the marathon. Time trials can be run on any measured course in training, but local races serve very well as time trials. A low-pressure six- or seven-mile race makes a perfect time trial a couple of weeks before a twenty-miler or a marathon.

"Pace work" and "tempo training" are usually used interchangeably to refer to running at race pace for a distance that is long enough to settle into the proper rhythm but is considerably less than race distances. You might finish an easy ten-mile run with a mile of tempo work, for example, during which you attempt to run at exactly the pace you want to use in the race toward which you are working. Races are exciting, and most contestants always start at too fast a pace. You are likely to find yourself running a full minute per mile faster than you had intended because of the starting line adrenaline rush. This can be disastrous in a race, and one of the best ways to counteract it is by doing training in which you concentrate on the exact pace you plan to use in the race. In training for a 2:40 marathon, for example, you might do a lot of tempo training during the last month at exactly a 6:00 per mile pace, depending on your race strategy. This would allow you to start the marathon at the right speed, rather than burning out by running the first five miles at 5:30's.

PULSE RATE TRAINING

One of the most accurate ways to gauge the real training effect of your current running is by using your pulse rate as an indicator. Too much attention to exact pulse rates before, during, and after exercise can become obsessive and is a waste of time; but occasionally checking your pulse can give you valuable information about your training. Some runners just can't be bothered with this rather mechanistic approach when they are running, and I must admit that I usually take this view myself. There is no doubt that the information is useful, though, and it would be far more instructive than the subjective notes I usually put in my training diary.

Electronic gadgets are the only really accurate way to get a pulse during strenuous exercise; but if you learn to take your pulse quickly after you stop running, you can get a fairly good reading. Practice taking rest pulses first—this will also tell you what your base is. The resting pulse is weaker and harder to find than a pulse during exercise; but it is slow, steady, and easy to count. Your basal pulse is best taken before you get out of bed, and your resting pulse while sitting or standing will be a few beats higher. Trained runners generally have lower pulses than the average adult figures of 70–80 beats per minute because of their increased stroke volume and output of blood during each contraction of the heart. Highly conditioned runners typically have resting pulse rates in the range of 40–60, with a few extending down into the 20's. (Women's pulse rates are typically about ten beats higher than men's at any given level of exercise.)

When you exercise hard, your pulse rises as the heart pumps more blood. It then falls again when you stop. Since the pulse

of the well-trained athlete falls back toward normal rather rapidly, you have to take the pulse very quickly after you stop
moving to get a reading that is anywhere near accurate. It is
virtually impossible to take a pulse by feel when you are actually running, but you can locate it with your fingers just before
you stop and then take it immediately after halting. The two
easiest locations to use are the radial artery on the thumb side
of the inner wrist and the carotid artery in the hollow of the
throat on either side of the neck. Count the pulse over a period
of six seconds and multiply by ten. By the end of a minute or
even fifteen seconds, the pulse will often have dropped a good
deal.

Your heart rate during exercise is a function of the intensity
of the exercise for *you*. Thus, a hill or a sprint that raises your
pulse to 175 is going to have more of a training effect than one
that raises it only to 150. In general, the rate will be higher as
you move through a training session, due to accumulated oxygen debt. Really serious athletes can use the effects of a particular workout to compare their training level from one season
to the next and adjust their workouts accordingly. If you finish
a particular workout (the same set of intervals run at the same
speed) with a pulse of 155 where it was 175 last year, you are
either in better shape or you have peaked sooner. You have to
decide which from your training. Lasse Viren's coaches use this
kind of data before major competition to decide whether he
needs more speed work (if he is not sharpened enough) or less
(if he is peaking too quickly).

Those of us who are less well trained and have more modest
aspirations than Viren can use the pulse we reach to determine
whether we are working hard enough, whether we need more
rest, and what sort of shape we are in. If you are trying to get a
hard workout, your pulse should get quite close to your maximum. (Remember that this is a recommendation for the runner who is already well trained, not the overweight beginner!)
Your maximum can be determined accurately only by testing
with instruments on a treadmill or similar device, but the rule
of thumb is that your maximum is roughly 220 minus your age.

This is only an average figure, but it will give you at least some idea of how closely a particular effort approaches your maximum. If you are 35 years old and get a pulse of 180 at the top of a long hill, you know you're working hard; if you get 125, you've been jogging.

Recovery rates tell you a lot about your condition. If you get close to your maximum rate during a hard run of a couple of miles and the pulse has dropped back to 20 or 30 beats over your resting rate within two or three minutes, you are getting into pretty good shape. If it takes ten minutes for the same result, your conditioning is not nearly as good. The particular figures in these examples are not important, but if you try this sort of test every couple of months or so, you will get an excellent notion of the effects of your training. If your recovery rate is improving during base training, and if it takes a harder run to get your heart rate up, you know that your training is working—these are far better indications than your time over a particular course.

Pulse rates from day to day can provide good clues as to the training you need. If you find that your resting pulse is ten beats higher than usual on the morning after a hard run, it means you haven't fully recovered and that you should take an easy day. An elevated pulse persisting from one day to the next is often a sign that you are overtraining or that you are fighting off an illness. Slow down!

HILLS

Hill training is one of the most versatile tools the runner has. Running hilly routes is obviously good specific training for races held on similar terrain, but it also strengthens many of the leg muscles beyond anything that can be managed by running on the flats and provides reserve capacity for your other runs. On steep hills, the quadriceps muscles at the front of the thigh are used far more than they are in normal running, and this is beneficial since these muscles often become weak in distance runners. Hill training at a moderate pace is recommended in this book as part of base training to increase aerobic capacity. Stiff hill training is used by many runners to build up strength before sharpening. Downhill running can also be used to help the runner to increase leg speed.

ALTITUDE TRAINING

Since there is less oxygen in the air at altitudes high above sea level, the body is forced to make a number of changes in acclimatizing to running at elevations above about 1200 meters (4000 feet). Many coaches and runners are convinced by experience that doing some training at higher altitudes is very helpful to overall performance. There is no doubt that runners who live at high altitudes do better in races that are also held at high altitude. Other training benefits can't be conclusively proven, but the experience of many runners seems to indicate that the advantages are real. Since the body is forced to process oxygen more efficiently at altitude, the value of running at altitude is easy to credit.

Altitude training is discussed in detail in Chapter IX. Only marginal effects are likely to be felt at elevations below 1500 meters (about 5000 feet), whereas above 3000 meters (10,000 feet) it will be difficult to run for extended periods at good speed, even after acclimatization. Altitudes somewhere in between therefore seem best suited for altitude training. Within this range higher elevations will generally stimulate more rapid acclimatizing effects but will also reduce your training pace. Because of the reduced pace at higher elevations, training both at altitude and at sea level seems to produce the best effects. Altitude training has been observed to be particularly beneficial to many racers who are not performing as well as they should. It also seems to bring runners of moderate experience more rapidly to a high level of efficiency.

RESISTANCE TRAINING

Resistance training is any type of exercise that involves more than the normal amount of resistance to the movement of the muscles. Weight lifting is resistance training, and so is running through surf. Many athletes believe that running in situations that increase resistance helps to build reserve strength so that they can train better and sustain fewer injuries. Running hills has already been mentioned. Running in sand, snow, or surf and running up sand dunes or gravel piles are other examples.

Special exercises like weight training are used by many coaches and athletes to prevent or treat injuries caused by muscle imbalances and also to strengthen particular muscle groups in both the upper and lower body in order to improve running. Whether such training is necessary is a matter of some controversy. Some strength training exercises are covered in Chapters VIII and XIV.

OTHER SPORTS AND ACTIVITIES

Many sports and activities other than running can provide excellent training, and there are good arguments for participating in a variety of activities, both to keep yourself fresh and to insure more balanced muscle development. Sports like cycling, swimming, cross-country skiing, handball, singles tennis, and basketball can provide a good cardiovascular workout if you play with enough vigor and if you have a high enough skill level. The latter reservation is important. I can't get a good workout playing tennis, for example, because I'm a lousy player; the volleys don't last long enough. With swimming, skiing, or cycling, though, I can get plenty of exercise. Obviously, these sports lack many of the advantages of running as training activities—especially its convenience—but they can be useful when you are coming off an injury. They are also helpful in preventing some injuries because they stress different groups of muscles from those used by the distance runner.

CHAPTER VI

ON THE ROAD:

Base Training

As ITS NAME implies, base training is the foundation of any running program. For the majority of dedicated distance runners, base training consists of thousands of miles on the roads and trails. Base training provides the underpinning for specific race training—the endurance that allows the runner to tolerate speed work and racing. It is also the source of most of the enjoyment derived from running. Base training has to be enjoyable for most runners, since it inevitably makes up the great bulk of their running experience. However bright the rewards of racing—even if it is your main motivation for running—the many miles in between races should be enjoyable, too. For the majority of the current crop of runners, though, it is the regular distance running of base training that provides most of the pleasure of the sport. Racing is good for an added fillip, but it's not the primary motivation for our daily runs.

The emphasis in this book is on extended mileage along the roads and trails during most of the year. This foundation is used to provide a strong aerobic base and a reserve of stamina and endurance that can sustain the runner during hard training and racing in selected seasons. This does not really mean that all the running of base training is long, slow distance, however. The really experienced runner who is already racing well should drop back from peak form to base training, but should certainly not be satisfied with merely jogging for three or four months. The emphasis for the already powerful runner is simply placed on distance, endurance, and stamina rather than on speed. The average training pace should be aerobic but not plodding.

For most dedicated runners who still have not even approached their best running potential, the base training period should bring on a steady improvement in both distance and speed. The point is that additional speed during base training should be allowed to come naturally rather than being forced. The runner should be building distance and training hard, but not drawing on deep reserves or trying to run all out. The difference between base training and sharpening is one of emphasis. The runner should understand what the primary objective of each period is: When you're racing, the object is to run as fast as you can; during sharpening, it's to build the speed needed for fast racing; in base training, the object is to become as fit as possible and to build a deep reserve of strength. The real test you should apply in deciding whether some particular element will fit well into your current stage of training is whether it will help or hinder in the particular objective you are working on now.

There is really a whole variety of techniques that can be used during the base training periods and a great number of ways in which they can be mixed. You should find a combination that's well suited to both your temperament and your needs, taking into account your past experience, your current goals, and your state of fitness. Certain training tactics work well at some times but not at others. Running weekly races at less than full effort might be fine at some stages; but it definitely doesn't fit in at a time when you are rapidly increasing mileage, or when you are just recuperating from a hard marathon.

BUILDING YOUR PROGRAM

Your plans for base training should be structured around the goal that you have set for a target, even though base training is the least specific of the various phases of training. Extended distance running is the staple of base training, whether you are working toward ultramarathons, five-mile road races, or even one-mile track contests. Your goals and what you intend to accomplish are important, however. If you are aiming toward short road races or track races, doing hundred-mile weeks will provide an excellent background, but you don't have to worry about your exact mileage totals in terms of exceeding a particular crash point as you do if you are aiming for longer distances. As with all aspects of training, your base training should be aimed toward limited goals during any particular time period. By concentrating on one objective at a time, you will often find that you can improve in a number of other areas as well, but if you take a scattergun approach and try to do everything at once, you are likely to accomplish nothing.

Distribution of daily mileage should be governed by your training phase. When you are building mileage rapidly, it is best to run about the same distance every day, except perhaps for a long run on one day of the weekend. If you have already leveled off at the distance you plan to maintain, it is better to run a variety of distances, a subject covered in more detail later in the chapter. It is difficult for most people to build mileage up very quickly if they use a hard/easy routine with big mileage differences between days.

Suppose you are currently doing 60 miles each week by running 9 miles a day, 5 days a week, with a 15-miler on Sunday and one day off. Increasing your daily mileage to 10 miles will be easier than doing 12 one day and 7 the next.

Hard/easy routines are discussed in somewhat more detail below, but during periods of rapidly increasing mileage, it seems best to run the same distance more briskly on the hard day, dropping to a more relaxed pace on recovery days. This has an additional advantage—if you need two recovery days because of the extra work load, you don't find yourself facing a double-mileage day when you still feel washed out. When you are building mileage, you are likely to find that long-mileage days put a lot of stress on your joints and tendons, which are hard pressed just to adapt to the overall increases in distance.

Similarly, though the inclusion of one extralong training run is an important element in base training, I don't think that you should try to extend this run at the same time you are trying to rapidly push up your overall mileage. Your legs will have a hard enough job adapting themselves to the stress of the extra mileage while you are building overall distance, and this is not the time to introduce an extended training run that is five or ten miles longer than you are used to doing. The best method is usually to hold your long run to the same mileage while you are increasing your daily distances and then to lengthen it when your weekly mileage has stabilized.

LOSING WEIGHT

If you need to lose weight as part of your overall training program, the time to do it is early in the base training period. You may not drop to perfect racing weight just then, but you should get close. Don't just rely on your extra mileage and later increases in speed to take off all the extra pounds. They may do so, but it is likely to take a long time. If you want your training to count and if you want to improve quickly in other areas, getting rid of the tummy folds is the first place to start. If you are going to make the effort of putting in over a hundred miles a week, it is silly to waste most of the effort in simply working off pounds. Building up either mileage or speed is much harder on your body when you are overweight, and you are more likely to run into overuse injuries. You also won't be able to train your legs to move efficiently at the pace you should, because your weight will slow you down so much.

At any given distance and level of effort, you will lose four to five seconds per mile for every couple of extra pounds you are carrying. This means that if you are running at 20 pounds over your racing weight, your pace at a particular energy output will be some 45 seconds slow. If you should be running easy 7:15's, you'll find yourself doing 8's instead. Your legs will not be learning to move efficiently at the faster pace, so when you go into your sharpening phase and finally take off the extra weight, you won't be able to exploit all that cardiovascular conditioning you have built up, because you just can't increase your leg speed that much without tying up. Everyone has to decide how fit he or she wants to become, of course, but if you're going to push hard for a goal like a fast marathon or a big hill climb, the most efficient start of the training program is to lose those extra pounds.

The only way to lose weight rapidly is to diet, using whatever scheme works best for you. Fasting, discussed in Chapter XIII, is the quickest way to lose weight and has been found useful by quite a few runners for other reasons as well. Simply reducing the quantities of food you eat is a standard method. It helps to chew your food slowly and thoroughly and to switch to a set of small dishes, taking no extra helpings. Concentrating on whole grains, vegetables, fresh fruit, and salads is a technique preferred by many runners. Avoid sweets, oils, and fats—especially in the evening, when running's depletion of your sugar supplies is likely to urge overconsumption of sugary foods. Fortunately for the serious runner, regular training greatly speeds up weight loss and eliminates many of the unpleasant side effects of dieting. A runner doing a regular ten miles a day in training will burn up an extra thousand calories a day beyond normal requirements, which translates into a pound of extra weight loss every three or four days.

Most runners find that they can train perfectly well while either dieting or fasting, though many cannot race. You should probably not try to rapidly increase mileage or other stress while you are losing weight quickly. Stick to your usual routine until you have lost your extra supply of fat. The results will be dramatic enough after you have lost your excess weight, more than making up for the time required to get rid of it.

TRAINING DISTANCE AND THE COLLAPSE POINT

Another fundamental principle in planning your base training has already been mentioned: Ken Young's formulation of the relationship between training mileage and the wall or collapse point. The wall is familiar to most serious runners, whether they have encountered it in race situations or not, since it is not uncommon to reach it on a long, fast training run. The wall is the point at which you run out of muscle glycogen and are forced to switch over almost entirely to fat metabolism, with a consequent slowing of pace. This is not the slight reduction in speed of a top racer during the last five miles of a marathon. A good marathoner slows a little because of the effects of pain and fatigue. When you hit the wall, your pace drops a full two minutes or more per mile! In training runs the wall is definitely noticeable, but it is not particularly painful, because you don't have to force yourself to maintain the fastest possible pace. Because you don't go through a special preparation and tapering period for a training run, you are likely to reach the collapse point earlier than you would in an important race when you try to schedule everything just right. By the time you hit the wall in a race of marathon length or longer, you've been running at top speed for a long way, and the wall really hurts.

One of the main functions of base training is to stimulate all the physiological changes that will extend your collapse point to longer and longer distances. These training effects are many. As your running becomes more efficient and you learn to relax even at a good pace, you use less energy to travel each mile, so your stored reserves last longer. As your oxygen uptake improves, through more efficient lungs, heart, blood, capillarization, and the ability of the muscle cells to extract oxygen, you are able to use more fat as fuel while running fast, so that the glycogen reserves stored in your muscles and liver can be stretched out for a longer period of time. There are a host of changes, but they add up to an ability to run farther before you run out of high-octane fuel and hit the wall.

Ken Young was the first person to come up with a simple formula relating base training to the collapse point, so that you can predict where you will encounter the wall, assuming optimum conditions. (If you run too fast, of course, you'll burn your reserves inefficiently and collapse sooner. The same qualifications apply if the course is exceptionally hilly compared with your training routes; if there is a bad headwind; if you've trained hard just before the race, so that you haven't had time to build up muscle glycogen stores; and so on. Young's formula gives you the *best* distance you can expect to run before reaching your collapse point.)

Young says that you should take the sum of the longest training distance you've run recently during a period of 60 consecutive days and divide by 20—that's your collapse point. Thus, if you've run 583 miles in the last two months, the wall is out around 29 miles for you if you do everything just right. Another way of stating the formula is that if you run regular mileage every week for at least two months, your collapse point is three times your daily average. You need to average nine miles a day, seven days a week, to be sure of avoiding the wall in a marathon, a little more if you want a reserve cushion.

Young's formula seems to work surprisingly well for most runners; usually when it doesn't there is an obvious reason. Environmental factors can cause extra stress, or the runner may make a mistake. There are a few qualifications and pitfalls that I think you should take into account when using the formula, which is a remarkably useful tool in planning base mileage in order to train for particular goals.

One important qualification relates to using training times as a basis for figuring collapse points. It will not work, as some have suggested, to assume that you can run a 3½-hour marathon by training an average of an hour and ten minutes a day. This is an 8-minute-mile pace, and if that is your goal, it is safe to assume that a lot of your training mileage will be run at slower speeds. You'll be running some 7-minute miles, but also a lot of 9-minute ones. On your long runs you'll probably sometimes drop to 10 minutes a mile or slower. The average will almost certainly be slower than your racing speed, probably about 9 minutes a mile; at this rate 70 minutes of running each day will cover only a little over 7¾ miles, and your collapse point will actually be at 23⅓. The same discrepancies will apply to faster runners as well. If you want to use time as a basis for figuring your collapse point, you need either to convert into a mileage equivalent or to allow extra training time. Generally the collapse point works out to be around 2½ times the average daily running time, but the relationship is not as precise as it is with distance.

Other important qualifications concern the type of course and pace. If you want to run a very hilly race, it is best to train on similar terrain during the last period of base running. If you do, the formula will work out just right, with no corrections. If you don't have similar courses available where you live, however, then in addition to doing appropriate hill training after building your base, you should allow some room for error when you figure your collapse point. Similarly, if you run a race too early during your sharpening phase, when you haven't yet become really efficient at higher speeds, you'll hit the wall early unless you have built an extra cushion into your base mileage.

The first step in designing your base training, then, is to decide what sort of weekly mileage you want to be running toward the middle and end of the base period in order to reach your current goal. If you haven't had much experience racing at the distance you are shooting for and if your usual weekly mileage isn't terribly high, you should design your base mileage around the distance, probably with a little extra to spare. Thus, if you have raced a few marathons and you have decided to do some concentrated training leading up to a good time in the next one, you should probably bring your distance up to the range of seventy to eighty miles a week early in base training and keep it there. A more experienced runner working for improvement in the marathon or any other distance might want to work up to a hundred miles a week or a little more to develop improved aerobic capacity and mechanical reserves as a base for serious sharpening later on. If you are looking toward ultramarathons, you will have to think carefully about your time goals, about how far you think you can reasonably build your base in a particular period, and therefore about how much of your race you will have to run beyond the wall. You won't run a hundred-miler at marathon speeds, but the length of time you can go before slowing radically will be based largely on your training distances.

INCREASING MILEAGE

You shouldn't plan to continue to build mileage during your entire period of base training. Mileage is the raw material of which base training is made, not its ultimate goal. You should pick a reasonable weekly figure for a particular cycle in your training that fits well with your goal, work up to it, and then start to improve the quality of your base training.

Remember that you should not normally increase your average running distance more than 10 percent each week. It is important to realize that extreme increases can cause injuries that will set your training back rather than advance it. This 10-percent figure may be a little conservative for those running relatively low weekly mileage, but it is rather high for those in the 70–80-mile-per-week category, so it is a realistic maximum to use in planning long-range increases. From week to week you should regulate your mileage by watching for the signs of overstress and backing off when you feel loggy or tired.

The primary exception to the 10-percent rule is the experienced runner who has reduced mileage during a rest period or for other reasons such as family commitments, job pressure, or just plain laziness. If you have been running for several years and have lots of background mileage, you will often find that you can safely make some fairly rapid initial increases before settling down to the 10-percent figure. Thus, if you have slacked off during the winter months to only 30 miles a week after running 100 steadily for a long time, you could probably work back up to 70 in a few weeks. This kind of increase requires extreme care, though. Any signs of overuse should prompt you to slow down and increase mileage more slowly. You may find that your joints won't tolerate too rapid a rise.

You should expect that your pace will remain relatively slow during periods when you are rapidly building up your distance. Speed will not usually get better while you are dealing with the stress of extra mileage; it will often decline. Accept this as normal and don't try to force too much work out of your legs. If your speed does improve without straining, it is a good sign, because it means that your mileage increases are well within your limits. Don't expect everything to get better at once though. Other improvements will come after you have leveled off in your weekly distance.

One of the functions of base training is to improve aerobic running capacity and efficiency. If you can currently run aerobic 7-minute miles, working to an aerobic running speed of 6:30's or 6:00's will be the best possible base with which to go into a sharpening phase of training. You aren't going to improve your aerobic speed while you are still raising mileage; you have to level off first. Pick your mileage target, build up to it early in base training, and then start working within that framework for the rest of the current period of base training. Greater mileage volume is fine, but it is not an end in itself. If you aren't already running high mileages, you'll be better off running good training at 80 or 90 miles a week than dragging yourself on up to 120 or 140. High mileage is a useful training tool, but a mania for mileage can be just as destructive as a mania for speed; you can only build up so much in any one season, and if all your adaptive capacity is used up in adjusting to additional mileage, you won't have anything left for the other phases of training. Rodgers, Shorter, and other top runners didn't start at high mileage and top racing; they got there through years of consistent work, a few steps at a time.

The logic of Ken Young's formula as a minimum standard is

fairly inescapable, however, for those who want to race well. If you are moving fast enough to have to rely on muscle and blood sugar for a lot of your fuel, you will not be able to miss hitting the wall unless you have been putting in the minimum training mileage for at least two consecutive months. Fifty miles a week, no matter how much "quality" training it contains, won't get you through a marathon without crashing, and all the six-minute miles at the beginning won't yield a good time if you drop to 9:30's for the last five miles.

SIGNS OF OVERSTRESS

Throughout your training, it is important to become sensitive to what is going on in your body. One of the most pleasant aspects of running in general is that you become in better tune with yourself physically, rather than having your senses dulled by lack of exercise, overeating, and other ills of modern living. Remember, though, that what you are doing in training is applying stress to your body in order to force it to adapt and become stronger. Too much stress applied too quickly will break you down. Fortunately, it is easy to avoid overwork, because you constantly receive feedback from your body that will tell you what is going on—if you pay attention. It is really not hard to regulate your training if you notice how you feel and draw the obvious connections with your current training schedule.

Most runners get into trouble because they ignore the relationship between day-to-day physical well-being and their training. If you feel great and have lots of bounce in your legs the day after a hard workout, then your program is working and you are within your limits. If you are tired and draggy even after a full night's sleep and your legs are mildly sore, you are working too hard and you should take a rest. It is really as simple as that. (Specific pains in the legs, such as a sore Achilles tendon or a burning feeling in a muscle, can be signs of general overuse or of specialized problems. See Chapter XIV.) Many runners ignore these obvious inferences because they have lived too long out of touch with their bodies and because they develop a misplaced ego involvement with their training schedules. It doesn't really show how tough you are if you keep up hard training despite clear signs of overstress; it shows how stupid you are!

The initial signs of overtraining are usually quite mild. Your body is trying to tell you to rest. The most common ones are:

1. Sore or aching legs. Strong localized pain indicates an actual injury, which should be treated before continuing training. A very mild general soreness or light ache persisting into the next day after a training run, though, is a sign that you have not yet recovered from your last session. You need rest, not a hard workout.

2. Changes in your normal physical rhythms and routines—fatigue, general malaise, irritability, insomnia or a need for much more sleep than usual, poor appetite, clumsiness, difficulty in concentrating, or a general washed-out feeling. You need rest, not a steeling of your willpower.

3. Vulnerability to colds and flu. Overtraining often leaves you susceptible to minor infections.

4. A higher-than-usual resting pulse. Your pulse will usually stay a little higher than normal for several hours after a hard run, during the period of initial recuperation. Persistence of a higher-than-usual pulse into the following day is a sign that you have not recovered from a workout. You should rest or take very easy runs until it is back to normal. (We are talking here about *your* normal pulse rate, which is generally much lower in a well-trained runner than in an average person. If your usual pulse on waking is 50 beats per minute, a pulse of 60 is higher than average and should prompt you to take an easy day. Really high rates or increases persisting for more than a couple of days indicate that you should consult a physician.)

5. A slump. If your performances are persistently poor for

several days in a row, it is a sign of overwork, not insufficient training. Back off.

All these signs are friendly warnings from your body that you are going to get into deep trouble if you don't slow down a little. Paying attention to them will allow you to increase at the maximum rate possible for you. This will be different at different times, and it is important to learn to accept this fact and to work with your body, not against it. You should feel good during your training: pleasantly tired after a hard workout, but not exhausted. You should bounce back quickly. Remember that all the great coaches of recent years have agreed that overwork is far more dangerous to the runner than inadequate training.

HARD/EASY PATTERNS

Another principle that is fundamental both in base training and during later phases of sharpening and racing is that of a regular rhythm of hard work and rest. Though the principle has been applied by many successful runners and coaches, it was best formulated by former Oregon track coach Bill Bowerman. Essentially, Bowerman says that there are far more overtrained runners than undertrained ones and that a hard workout has to be followed by an easy one in order to allow the body to recuperate from the stress and for the runner to improve. Bowerman was not a slave to a particular pattern and noted that some runners recover faster than others, so that hard/easy patterns have to be individualized to match the athlete's own cycles. Rapid recuperation time is not necessarily characteristic of the best runners, so there is no sense in allowing your ego to become involved when you analyze the amount of recuperation time you need. Steve Prefontaine, one of Bowerman's pupils and one of the best distance men in the United States until his untimely death, needed two easy days after a hard workout. Some runners can tolerate two hard days between easy ones. But Bowerman's rule of thumb that you should alternate hard and easy workouts is the best one to start with.

The root of this principle should never be ignored. The whole idea of training is to stress the body, breaking down some tissue and pushing your muscles to work hard so that they will be stimulated to grow back stronger, better coordinated, and able to deal with still greater stress. This is a cycle like the tides, not a linear progression like climbing a ladder. There are two equally essential parts to the whole, and if either is removed training won't take place. The first part is the stress, which is essential as a stimulus to the body. The second part is the recuperation stage, during which the actual rebuilding takes place. If you remove the stress, the body won't bother to get stronger. If you remove the rest phase, it won't be able to. Though there are many cycles operating at different rates in the body, it has been shown time and again that rebuilding after a hard workout normally requires more than a day. This means that hard workouts should be alternated with easy days during which the body actually strengthens itself.

When you are doing speedwork, the application of this principle is fairly obvious—you do only two or three hard interval sessions a week. The mixture during base training is less clear, and it will vary somewhat from one month to the next. During stages when mileage is being built up and the daily runs are generally about the same distance, a hard/easy sequence simply boils down to running a bit harder one day and easing off somewhat for the next day or two. When adding mileage rapidly, you should avoid running too hard, anyway. The added mileage is usually enough stress, so that one or two runs a week that approach your aerobic limits are usually plenty. As your distance levels off, you should introduce more variety both in distance and speed, and you will have to learn to be sensitive to those workouts that are tough and those that are easy.

The first few times you do a run of twenty-five to thirty miles, for example, it will certainly be a hard workout no matter how slowly you run it, and you should plan an easy day or two afterward. Later on, as you become more fit, you are likely to find that a long run at the end of the week is really relaxing, providing you maintain a moderate pace; so you may be ready for a brisk ten miles the next day. Similarly, if you start running on hilly trails after a long period on the flats, the workout will be a hard one even though you don't attack the hills. After you have been running hills regularly for a couple of months, you may find that a relaxed run in the hills is a good way to recuperate from the effects of a flat run near your aerobic limits. For a strong hill runner, only Lydiard-style springing, or heavy *fartlek* on the trails, will turn the hills into a hard day.

AEROBIC RUNNING

The crucial point to remember about base training is that it is designed to improve your aerobic capacity, as well as endurance, stamina, and the toughness of the mechanical systems of your body. One of the major contributions that Arthur Lydiard has made to training theory is insisting that each phase of training should be viewed as a discrete part that has a particular purpose, and that the runner should stick to one primary objective at a time. During the base period, you should not introduce a lot of anaerobic or oxygen-debt training. You may do some surging occasionally or run up a hill as though you mean it, but you should not go out and do a bunch of 220's or hill sprints as hard as you can go. Save it, so that you will really want to push hard when the time comes.

It is important to note, however, that Lydiard's distance running during the base training period is not static and unchanging. You may start your base training period averaging only 8 to 9 minutes per mile, but if your base training is any good, you should not stay at that pace for month after month. Once your mileage has leveled off, your aerobic pace should gradually improve, though the rapidity and amount of improvement will depend very much on your experience and your starting level.

To improve your aerobic pace it is important to develop a good feel for different levels of effort during aerobic running. Most descriptions of particular paces are rather subjective and depend a lot on both the ability and the experience of the runner. Even the now-familiar "talk test"—the ability to carry on a conversation while running—is ambiguous. Does it mean that you can rattle on with no more interruption for breath than you would have to make while talking over a beer, or does it mean that you can talk without gasping for breath between each few words? The implications are different for one runner than they are for another, and the variations are important. Long, slow distance—running along at a bit better than a jog, but still at a relaxed pace—is one of the staples of base training, but it should not be the only one, especially for good runners who have lots of mileage behind them but don't have much experience with racing and speedwork.

Once you have reached the distance level at which you want to train for the next couple of months, you should begin to experiment both with varying distance and with changes in pace. Some of the techniques discussed below, like surging, are useful in this respect, as are long runs once a week and runs on hilly trails. One important factor, though, is to explore your aerobic pace limits at different distances. Don't go into oxygen debt in these sessions, and don't do real speedwork, trying to push yourself harder and harder. I would suggest that you not take any runs of less than five miles near your aerobic limit.

It is worthwhile to do about one run a week where you concentrate on staying at a stiff pace that requires you to breathe fairly hard. Don't start panting, and don't run so hard that you finish the run as if it were a race or a hard speed workout. You shouldn't be wrung out or exhausted. Nor should you slow badly at the end of the run because you have been running too hard. The distance should be shorter than your average daily run, perhaps five to seven miles. You shouldn't be racing or running your best time for the distance, but these should not be runs where you spend a lot of time looking at the scenery and letting your mind wander pleasantly. Run with your mind on your technique and your pace. Push your aerobic limit. This should be a good workout, though you should still finish it feeling as though you could turn around and run the course again, at a slower pace but not a survival trot. Clearly this is a hard workout, so you should have easy distance runs the day before and the day after. It isn't necessary to get any exact pacing times for such runs; the idea is not to achieve your top speed but to gradually push up your easy aerobic pace over a period of months. For this reason, it is probably best not to run these sessions on a track nor to time them very rigorously.

MIXING UP YOUR MILEAGE

Though a relatively even daily mileage is advisable when you are building up your regular distance rapidly, it is not the most effective way to train once you have stabilized your weekly distance. Variations in distance provide a variety in types of stress on the body and are likely to result in more balanced development. Your exact schedule will naturally vary with your own circumstances, and you may choose to run even mileage except for a long weekend run, just because that is what fits your own schedule. If you have the chance, though, variety is a good idea. A runner doing eighty miles a week regularly might set up a schedule like this.

Sunday	*Monday*	*Tuesday*	*Wednesday*
20-mile road run, moderate pace	7 miles, easy	12 miles on roads, moderate effort, some *fartlek*	7 miles, good effort, near aerobic limit

Thursday	*Friday*	*Saturday*	
10 miles, easy	12 miles on trails at moderate effort	12 miles easy on roads	

This example provides variety and hence gives more balanced training and more enjoyable running than identical runs every day. It includes one long run a week, a schedule that generally follows a hard/easy pattern, and one short run that is intended to push the runner's aerobic limits. The harder features should not all be introduced at the same time, however. Thus, a runner who has just reached eighty miles a week might begin by working in a long run on one day of the weekend, following it with a short, easy day for recuperation. After a few weeks, some hilly trail running could be added once a week, and so on. These variations help your body to learn to deal with different types of stress, and at the same time lend interest to your training.

Note that easy days are not necessarily low-mileage days. For the experienced runner who is running at a steady mileage every week, a ten-mile run at a moderate pace can be quite relaxing and can speed up healing in the legs after a hard day. Emphasizing different types of stress on succeeding days can also help to balance your schedule without overdoing things. In the example just used, a fast, short run follows one with some *fartlek*—neither one a really easy day. Such a sequence often works out fairly well, as long as you are careful to cut back whenever you notice signs of overstress.

The long weekly run in the schedule above is a particularly important element in the training of anyone who wants to race distances of twenty miles or more. Even though overall training mileage is the most important factor in allowing you to run a long way without hitting the wall, extended aerobic runs play an important part, too. They teach the body to actually maintain a high level of energy output for long periods, and you learn how to pace yourself during such runs. Once you have gotten used to them, I think you will find that these runs are among the most enjoyable features of your training. They should not normally be run at a fast pace—you are not trying to reproduce the stresses of racing—but some of them should be run at your usual training pace for as long as you can comfortably maintain it. At first you are likely to find that you slow down during the last few miles; but as your limits are extended, you will have no difficulty in running twenty to thirty miles comfortably.

The actual length of your long runs should be commensurate with both your overall training mileage and your goals. If you are planning on racing long-distance, you should cover your race distance occasionally, even if the pace has to be quite slow. Marathoners should run 26 miles a few times before actually racing the distance. If you are training only 65–75 miles a week, you should not run the full marathon distance often, but going the length of the race occasionally will help the body to adapt to the special effort of extended running. It is also a great psychological boost to have actually run the distance before, so that you can concentrate on pacing in a race, rather than coping with lingering doubts about your capacity to run that far.

Those training at regular distances in the neighborhood of 100 miles a week should run at least 25 miles on the weekend run, once they have become used to the overall weekly routine. Thirty-mile runs should be done occasionally. Such long runs develop the capacity of the body to utilize fat for fuel more effectively, so that muscle glycogen supplies will last longer.

If you are running 100 miles a week or more, you should also consider breaking your daily mileage into two runs at least some of the time. Most serious runners find that two 7-mile runs, for example, have a better training effect than a single 14-miler. Whether this is feasible depends on your personal schedule and preferences—running twice a day inevitably takes more time than a single run, because of dressing, showering, and warm-up time. The following week might be used by a runner who had been doing 100-mile weeks for some time.

Sunday	Monday	Tuesday	Wednesday
MORNING: 25-mile run, moderate pace EVENING:	10 miles, easy	7 miles, hilly trails	10 miles, easy
		7 miles on roads, sharp pace	

Thursday	Friday	Saturday
MORNING:		
7 miles, *fartlek*	10 miles, easy	7 miles, hilly trails
EVENING:		
10 miles, comfortable pace		7 miles, moderate pace

The long weekly run should not be broken into two sessions, since this would defeat the purpose.

VARYING YOUR PACE

While you should avoid any real speed work during base training, some variations in pace and style can be helpful, both to improve your aerobic pace and to teach you to run more efficiently. Grinding along at exactly the same tempo every day can become boring and allow your body to slump into staleness. The use of some faster aerobic running has already been mentioned, and other changes of pace like hills and trail running are discussed below. Some variations during your regular runs are beneficial and fun as well, so long as you don't try to push too hard.

These changes are described in the accompanying schedules as *fartlek*, though the term is used loosely here. *Fartlek* is most correctly used to describe fairly intense interval-style work on the trails, and this type of training should be left for sharpening periods. A more moderate version is very pleasant and helpful for varying some of your daily runs, however. Use a lot of changes in pace and experiment with varied style, not trying to discipline yourself, but experimenting with different movements. Thus, you might try intensifying your effort for a brief period by springing for fifty paces or so, pushing hard off your toes and swinging your arms high, bounding well off the ground with each step. Experiment also with running as lightly as possible, tucking your rear end forward and trying to land very lightly on your feet, almost slithering along the ground and relaxing as much as possible.

One excellent variation is surging. Pick a spot fifty yards or so down the road, and when you reach it, slowly begin to pick up your pace, gradually moving faster and faster—but concentrate on staying very relaxed and maintaining the most efficient stride possible. When you begin to tie up and lose your relaxation, slow down again. This is an excellent way to start learning how to run faster without tensing up. As you near the end of your base training period, try maintaining some of these surges over longer periods to begin developing your leg speed.

You should also experiment with methods of relaxing during your runs. Try various ways of stretching your arms and upper body while you are running. This can be a great aid during long races, when the upper body tends to become tense and rigid as fatigue sets in. Rolling your arms over your head and behind your back provides a good stretch. Letting your arms hang loosely and flop about for several paces is also good. These flopping runs are usually called "shakedowns" in track routines.

In experimenting with your pace, remember that a faster, lighter stride is the most efficient. Though the stride naturally lengthens somewhat as you run faster, intentionally taking longer strides is not the most efficient way to run. The best runners move up and down very little as they run, and their strides are short and quick. Their heads and centers of gravity move almost straight forward.

HILLS

Hill running can be used for a number of different purposes during different phases of training. Lydiard and many of his followers use very intensive hill training to build strength in the legs before sharpening with speed work. This and other types of hill training are discussed in detail in the next chapter. Hill running should be discussed briefly here, though, because extensive work in the hills makes excellent base training.

One of the great advantages of running long hills during base training is that they provide a superb aerobic foundation—just what base training is supposed to do. Running a long, steep hill imposes heavy demands on the lungs and cardiovascular system even when you go very slowly. Since it puts very different types of stress on the legs than does running on the flats, it helps to balance the muscular development of the legs and to avoid the overuse injuries that result from running too fast too soon. Further discussion of both the advantages and disadvantages of hill running will be postponed until the next chapter.

It is important to note here that you should not do a lot of sharp training on the hills until the end of base training. The hill training used to begin the sharpening process normally concentrates on sprinting up hills or on springing up them with a strong push off the toes and a high leg lift, as Lydiard teaches. In other words, it is heavy anaerobic work that is also designed to provide intense resistance to strengthen the legs. What you should do during base training is to run the hills near your aerobic limit. Long hills are excellent earlier in base training, because you have to slow down to keep going, producing sustained work for the cardiopulmonary system. Short hills can be run in oxygen debt which is repaid on the other side, but these should be treated very circumspectly during the early phases of base training.

Runners who have done lots of hill running in the past can simply do some hilly runs as part of their normal weekly routine. During base training I do about half my runs on steep trails. If you have not done much hill work, however, you will find that they impose a lot of stress at first. You should therefore leave them alone while you are building up mileage. Wait until you have leveled off in distance for several weeks, and then try running a hilly course once a week or so. The longer and steeper the hills, the better, since they will force you to keep the pace slow. Until your legs are used to the hills, run the downhills lightly and slowly, concentrating on reducing the impact on your knees. Don't run hills without warming up thoroughly, and avoid them if you are having any Achilles tendon or quadriceps trouble. (The Achilles tendon is the tendon connecting your calf muscle to your heel; the quadriceps are the muscles at the front of the thigh.)

The trails and hills are inseparable for me, because they go together in the area where I live—the trails are mountain trails. Trails are usually at least slightly hilly, and they make ideal training ground near the end of base training, combining hills of varied length. If you run them fast, they make a perfectly varied workout. Taken in a more relaxed way, however, trails are good any time during base training. The more natural surfaces are not so hard on the legs, once you are used to them; and changing terrain results in more balanced muscle development, which helps to prevent injuries. Rough trails can pose some real problems for those not used to them, however, since running habits learned on the roads can lead to a misstep and a sprained ankle.

The first few times you run on trails, unless they are unusually smooth, you should jog slowly to learn good foot placement and to see how well suited your shoes are for trail running. Foot placement on rough terrain during fast running is a technique that comes only with practice. When the footing is tricky, you have to watch the trail, looking at the scenery only after you have unconsciously memorized the footing in the next few yards. When you are watching the trail, you also need to be careful about running into overhanging branches. A twig that isn't large enough to catch your peripheral vision can be dangerous to your eyes. Running shoes that are excellent for pounding along the roads are not always stable enough to be suitable for the trails. Some shoes are quite sloppy when you step on a sidehill, so that on rough ground your ankle will be twisted off to the side without warning. The tread design is not really very critical for trail running, but lateral stability on varied surfaces is vital.

You are likely to find yourself tripping rather frequently the first time you run a rough trail, until you get used to lifting your feet higher to clear obstacles. Be especially careful when you begin to get tired, since the hip flexors that lift the legs are usually the first muscles to fatigue. It's easy to catch your toe and go sprawling when this happens. The skinned hands that result aren't a serious injury, of course, but they aren't much fun, either.

Aside from the training benefits, trail runs provide the most inspiring experiences in the sport. No other pleasure in running (and few others in life) can compare to the freshness of the sunrise on a spring trail run or the crackling of the leaves underfoot on a crisp fall afternoon as you run through the autumn golds, oranges, and reds on a forest trail.

FINDING YOUR OWN WAY

When you read the recommendations in this book or any other, it is important to remember that no one can give you definitive answers about every aspect of your training. One of the worst training errors that you can make is to follow someone else's program slavishly, expecting your body to respond just the way another person's did. Even assuming that a training program was worked out in a truly scientific manner for a large group of top athletes, there would be no guarantee that it would be a good regimen for the next person who came along.

Consider the matter of differing muscle composition, for example. We don't know how fixed the percentages of slow- and fast-twitch fibers in the muscle tissue are, so we don't know whether particular types of training might change these percentages. Even if they are genetically fixed, however, it might well be that one type of training would be more effective for an individual with a high percentage of slow-twitch fibers, while another program would be better for someone with a higher percentage of fast-twitch ones. The person with a larger number of slow-twitch fibers might require more speed training to synchronize the recruitment of motor units and perhaps to speed contractile movement, while the person with a greater number of fast-twitch fibers might need far more aerobic training to improve the muscles' ability to process oxygen.

This particular example is purely speculative, and it is only one of hundreds of variations that exist between different people. The point is that you have to pay a lot of attention to what is happening to your own body and to relate it to the experience you have had in the past. The training theories in this book are intended to provide a useful framework in which to interpret some of what happens in your own training, but it is only by finding out how your own body reacts to different types of stress that you will be able to gradually refine your training and achieve results that are more satisfactory to you.

CHAPTER VII

HILL RUNNING

THIS CHAPTER SHOULD bear a cautionary label similar to those used for drugs having potent effects on the body. WARNING: *The author is habitually addicted to running hills, and his objectivity is therefore suspect regarding the topic.* Besides enjoying the hilly trail runs that compose most of my favorite courses, I am convinced that hill running provides some of the best possible training for other kinds of running. The racer can train without hills, of course, but I think that hills are among the best training tools the runner has, in addition to providing many special challenges and pleasures. Hills lend variety to the sport, increasing the physical difficulty of running, the intellectual challenge of pacing yourself, the technical problems of efficient style on both uphill and downhill sections, and the added complexity of racing tactics for competition held on hilly courses.

TRAINING ADVANTAGES

Hill running can be used as a training technique in a number of ways. Lydiard and his followers like Ron Dawes use intensive hill running as a strength-building tool and toughener to begin the period of sharpening and speed work. I feel that once you have built up enough background mileage so that your legs can tolerate the additional stress, you can benefit from extensive hill running throughout the base conditioning period. There are some special advantages to running hills that can far outweigh the disadvantages discussed below.

Hills provide a natural form of resistance training for the legs, working only against body weight in a natural running action. As a result, the runner can gain many of the advantages of strengthening exercises while actually running, rather than working on weight machines and the like. Reserve power is built up which can make muscle pulls during speed training less likely and can serve as an excellent reserve against the fatigue that often slows the runner in the later stages of a long race. Running up hills places particular demands on some of the muscles that are often weak enough to cause problems for runners: the quadriceps, hip flexors, and the front muscles of the lower leg. Weak quads often contribute to muscle pulls and knee problems in distance runners. These are the driving muscles for hill climbing and are greatly strengthened by regular hill runs. The hip flexors, which raise the legs at the hips, are usually the first muscles to fatigue in a race, so that the runner stumbles easily over the smallest bumps and loses stride length. Because you have to lift your legs much higher when you are running up a hill than you do on the flat, the hip flexors gain strength and endurance. The hip flexors get special benefit when you run steep, rocky trails on which you have to lift your feet high to clear obstacles. Similarly, many of the stabilizing muscles in the legs and feet receive much more use on hilly and uneven terrain than they do on flat, level running and are strengthened as a result.

But I think that one of the main advantages to hill running, whether it is done on trails or paved surfaces, is that the runner can reach a state of very high oxygen demand and energy output without having to push very fast. The danger of injury produced by excessive speed work at too early a stage can thus be avoided. At the same time, the pounding on the joints and connective tissue that produces overuse injuries is greatly reduced during uphill running. In fact, on a steep hill the runner can easily push to maximum oxygen demand while maintaining a light, relaxed stride.

Hill training is not a magic talisman that will produce results unobtainable in any other way, but I think that the runner who does extensive hill running as a part of base training will be able to develop better reserves, more strength, and increased endurance prior to sharpening and speed work than would be possible by training only on the flats. It is easier to develop these capacities early by running hills than by any other means. The benefits for any racer who plans on competing over hilly courses are simply a bonus.

THE OTHER SIDE OF THE COIN

There are also a few real problems associated with hill training that persuade some runners to avoid it. While I feel that most of these difficulties are easy to overcome, they should be mentioned here along with the advantages. The most important disadvantage is directly related to the positive side of hill training. Because of the additional stress imposed on a number of muscles, runners with active tendon or muscle problems should avoid hill training. This is particularly true if you are recovering from an injury in the calf muscle, the Achilles tendon, the quadriceps, or a deep groin muscle. Sufferers from shinsplints ought to stay away from the hills until they have recovered completely, too. More generally, you should recognize that hill training is potent medicine that has to be taken in reasonable doses. Starting hill training while you are pushing hard in several other ways is likely to cause trouble. Though uphill running is essentially a useful form of stress when it is used properly, descents do have significant hazards. It is the downhill running that brings most complaints about hill training. There is a distinct pounding when you run downhill that can be only partly alleviated by good technique. The impact is especially pronounced on steep slopes, and it is hardest on the knees, already the places that are most vulnerable to injury in distance runners. And though there are distinct advantages in learning downhill running techniques for races that involve hills, this is not a persuasive reason for using extensive hill running during the base training period.

Some runners I know arrange to run long uphill training runs and to be picked up at the top. But besides being logistically difficult, this method is possible only in mountainous regions where you can find steady hills at least a few miles long.

Many of the disadvantages of downhill running can be avoided if you relax on the descents and don't try to run fast, except during periods when you are actually training for hill technique in racing. By running the downhills at an easy pace, you can learn to reduce the impact of your footstrike during descents. This relaxed style will also serve you in good stead when you begin working on downhill speed. During the early stage of base training when I have not been running hills regularly, I always jog the downhill sections or run them at a relaxed pace to minimize strain on my knees and antigravity muscles. Later on, as my legs become more used to the hills, I run them faster.

One point worth noting is that many people who have had trouble with their knees have found that hill running gradually strengthens them, provided they don't try to increase stress too fast. I used to have a lot of trouble with my knees because of old skiing and football injuries, and downhills caused me real problems. Yet over a period of a couple of years of hill training, my knees got much stronger. Quite a few other runners have had similar experiences. Obviously, this will not be true in all cases, and you should be very cautious about hill running if you have knee trouble. But you shouldn't assume that you can't run hills just because of old knee problems—it may actually be beneficial, if you're sensible in building up your tolerance and not ignoring pain.

FINDING THE HILLS

There is a tremendous variety in hills, of course, and a corresponding diversity in what various runners mean when they talk about running hills. For some, any hundred-foot rise in the elevation of a course constitutes a significant hill, while road runners who live in naturally hilly terrain take such variations in stride as part of a normal "flat" circuit. A road climbing several miles at a 5- or 6-percent incline (3°–3.6°) will challenge any runner, but the pace will be very different from the one used to climb a steep mountain trail. If you are climbing a long, steep trail, you will naturally have to use a slower pace than you would on a milder grade. Short, steep hills run in repetition or on a rolling course have the effect of bringing on oxygen debt sooner if you maintain a fast pace. The training stimulus of the steeper hill is similar to that of a faster pace in sprint intervals; heavy demand is placed both on your strength and on your oxygen supply system.

Runners who live near rugged terrain will have their choice of many hills: short, long, gradual, and steep. Those who live in flatter regions will probably have to take what they can find. There are nearly always some hilly courses about, though, even if you have to take out a pair of hedge clippers and develop your own cross-country course, dropping down into washes and gullies and climbing little ridge lines.

In rural areas hilly roads are often the best ones for running, since they are usually the smallest and least-developed thoroughfares, for which large bridges have not been built to span drainages nor cuts made through every hill. Back roads and farm roads often have lots of steep dips and little traffic. Runners who live in areas with little vertical relief may have to content themselves with doing an occasional hill workout using repetitions up a single slope. If nothing else is available, the embankments around freeway interchanges will provide short, steep hills for repeat workouts.

If you are lucky enough to live in a place with a variety of hills, you should run different kinds. Long, steady grades that last for several miles are ideal for building stamina and endurance. They necessarily have to be run at a relatively slow pace, though you will find your time dropping rapidly as you get into condition. Be cautious about these if you've been doing a lot of fast running on the flats; you'll find the hills tough at first, and you'll need to lower your expectations. You may find yourself being run into the ground by someone who does regular hill training, though the same person would be much slower than you are on a more level course. I think that long, steady grades run at a moderate effort are particularly good in the earlier stages of base training. You are less likely to push too hard and risk injury on a seemingly endless hill than on shorter, intermittent climbs.

A hilly road or trail makes a useful training run later on in base training when you are stronger, providing repeated sections of high demand on the uphills and relaxation on the level sections and downhills. A route with substantial rises and tough gradients is best. If the hills aren't long enough and steep enough to really slow you down, they make the course harder, but don't serve the hill training function very well. Some of the hills should be at least a quarter-mile long and reasonably steep. The ideal course, if you can find it, is a steep hill that goes on for a couple of miles, followed by a rolling course with lots of shorter hills. The route of this type that is my own favorite begins by climbing a little over a thousand feet in the first three miles, with only a few brief flat spots and downhills. Then in the next eight miles there are alternating climbs, descents, and flat sections, with a total elevation gain in the uphills of an additional 1600 feet. If you can run a course like this two or three times a week during the latter phases of base training, you'll find routes like that of the Boston Marathon to be practically flat.

DIFFERENT TRAINING TECHNIQUES

Hills during base training should be run in the same general style as other base running. You should work hard on some days, but not put in much all-out effort, particularly over short distances. Sprinting up short hills, especially during the early stages of base training, is a bad idea. You are after long, steady effort, which will make you gradually stronger and stronger. You should find that hills become far easier over a period of months, so that you are easily charging up slopes that would have exhausted you at the beginning, but all-out interval-style effort should be left until the end of base training.

The reason that most runners should avoid rolling courses with a lot of short, steep hills during the early part of base training is that the uphills will almost certainly be very strenuous at that time, so that you will work too hard at them. If you are already a strong hill runner, this may not be the case, and rolling courses may be fine. Most runners should introduce hills into their base training with very long grades, though, making the effort one of endurance rather than hard intervals.

Two or three hilly runs a week are excellent during the later stages of base training. By this time a long, rolling course with as many hills as possible is ideal. You should still be running in such a way that you are not putting maximum effort into the hills, though. If you come back wiped out from a hilly run, slack off for a few days, and try running it a little more slowly next time. The combination of three days of hills, three days of flatter ground, and one day with a very long run is about right.

At the end of base training when you are starting your sharpening prior to moving into speed work, you can follow this same schedule, but the hill work should become intense. The alternate days on the flats should become easy days of relaxed running, but the hills should be run hard, repeatedly bringing you into severe oxygen debt. This can be done in a number of ways. If you have a course with enough steep hills, then running it with the correct pacing makes perfect hill training. The idea is to run the uphills hard, coast a little at the crests and the flats, maintaining speed and striding rather than dropping to a jog, but allowing yourself to recuperate. Run the downhills fast, learning downhill running technique, so that you can run fast without tying up. You'll have to keep breathing hard all the way down, but you will repay some of your oxygen debt in the process.

If you don't have a course with enough hills concentrated along it to be able to manage to get a hard workout this way, you'll have to do your hill training on a single local hill, running up and down it. This method is superb for controlling your training, and you're not likely to get bored during difficult workouts like this. Some people have a hard time getting themselves out for a workout on a single hill, though. If you find this to be a problem, it's a good idea to schedule these workouts with a reliable friend at the same stage of training, so you can provide one another with moral support.

Try to find a reasonably steep hill that is between a quarter-mile and a half-mile long. A good sequence is to run up the hill as hard as you can, then turn and run down at full speed, learning to recuperate on the downhill by using gravity and relaxing, not by running slowly. Keep up a good pace at the bottom of the hill, maintaining an even stride out onto the flat for some distance. If you can do so, then you have recovered from most of your oxygen debt during the downhill. It won't be possible to maintain full pace at first, but keep working on it. Jog on out from the hill a little farther, jog back to the bottom, and repeat the whole sequence. The number of repetitions will naturally depend on the length of the hill, on your general conditioning, and on how far into hill training you are. You may not be able to manage more than a half-dozen repetitions at the beginning, but you should work up to at least twice that. Go for an easy run at the end of the hill workout.

You will probably also have to begin your hill workouts by running less than the full length of the hill. Since the idea is to run the hill hard and then to run the downhill fast as well, it is better to turn around at 220 yards than to stagger exhaustedly on up. Find a good starting distance by experimentation, but run up to a specific mark at each repetition, rather than making it too easy by just running up until you feel like turning back. Pacing on uphills is one of the valuable lessons you can learn from hill training, and you won't learn it unless you are pushing up to a specific spot. The length should be gradually extended until you are running hills at least a third of a mile long.

If you don't have a long enough hill near your house, you can use some variation of Lydiard's hill training method, bounding up the hill with a strong takeoff from the toes and high knee and arm lift, making only a little progress at each step. This is a strenuous exercise, and you can push yourself to exhaustion even on a very short hill. Use it with care at first, though, since it is hard on the calf muscles and the Achilles tendons. Run down fast and keep going past the bottom of the hill, just as with regular hill intervals, maintaining your speed for a quarter-mile from the hill. Jog back and bound up again.

UPHILL AND DOWNHILL TECHNIQUES

Efficient uphill technique uses a short stride, full flattening of the heel on all but the steepest terrain, and an arm swing that is not exaggerated. A hard arm swing or an attempt to drive hard off the toe wastes energy. These methods are confined to sprinting, so that you may use them during a hard hill training session or as a tactic to demoralize an opponent during a race; but the cost is severe, so they should never be used as part of a normal climbing stride. If you want to speed up, take faster steps rather than trying to lengthen your stride. You can speed yourself up by consciously pumping your arms faster, so that your legs will match the cadence and speed up as well, but don't try to pump the arms hard. Similarly, a slightly higher knee lift will come naturally as you speed up, but the most efficient hill runners use a low knee lift and a fast pace.

Most runners will have trouble flattening their feet on steep hills, because their calves are too tight. Running uphill on your toes is tiring and very hard on the calves, which are deprived of the brief rest period they normally get during the heel-plant phase of your stride. It is particularly important to do plenty of stretching to make the calves more supple when you are doing hill training, both to promote efficient running and to avoid injury. Hill training puts a lot of stress on the calves and Achilles tendons even with good running technique, and they will tighten up badly if you don't make a point of stretching them well. You should sink to the heel at each step except on the very steepest mountain trails.

Good downhill technique is more difficult to learn than uphill style. But while strength on the ascent is largely a function of strength and stamina, effective downhill running is almost pure technique. Most runners don't do well on downhills because they haven't taken the time to refine their style. Anyone can run downhill, after all, and anyone can run it fast. Most racers tie up on the downhills, however, so that they either slow down or work a lot harder than necessary. They also suffer a lot of pounding on the downhills if they try to run fast, as well as using too much energy. All these stresses will take their toll later in the race.

You can start working on your downhill technique from the time you begin adding hilly courses to your base running. Relax! Let gravity do the work. Don't land stiff legged with a bang at every step—it's hard on the joints and slows you down. As mentioned before, you shouldn't try to run the downhills fast when you start running hills. Wait until your legs have become strong enough. You should work on a relaxed and fluid downhill style, however, flowing down the hills even when you are going quite slowly. Carry your arms fairly low to help maintain balance, and make sure you relax your abdomen and belly-breathe. Tensing your stomach muscles prevents your running smoothly and is likely to result in a stitch.

When you progress to faster downhill running, the key element is still relaxation. Gravity will pull you down the hill, and all you really have to do is to move your legs fast enough to keep up. On steeper hills, your speed is governed by the position of your center of gravity over your legs. If you lean forward, you will go faster, moving your legs more quickly to keep up. If you lean back, your legs will hit harder and brake your descent. Try to learn to speed up gradually without losing your relaxed position. You should land with your knees slightly flexed, so that shock is absorbed by a little give in the leg, just as it is on the flat. One reason for training with a lot of uphill before trying to run fast downhill is to strengthen the front muscles of the thigh enough so that they can act as shock absorbers in this way. As you get tired, you naturally try to take the stress off the quadriceps by landing straight legged. This is hard on the knees and the rest of the body. When you catch yourself doing this in training, slow down on the descents. In a race, try to stay relaxed, run fast downhill, and land on flexed legs.

The object of downhill training is to learn to run at full speed on the downhills while still relaxing and recuperating from a full effort on the ascents. A lot of races can be won on the hills. With good hill training, you'll find that you'll easily climb past those who haven't trained enough on the hills. On the downhills you can eat up both the runners who pushed too hard to maintain their pace on the climb and even some really strong runners who are so tough at climbing that they never practice for the downhills.

TRAIL RUNNING

The main difference between running hilly trails and running any other hilly course is that trails are more pleasant and have more variety. Trails with many hills are typically rather rugged, however, with irregular surfaces, protruding rocks, loose gravel, holes, tree stumps, overhanging branches, and similar obstacles being the rule rather than the exception. Foot placement is a crucial factor in this type of running, both for safety and as an essential racing technique if you do competitive running on the trails.

Never run on rough trails with unstable shoes. Some shoes will hold your foot steady when you step on a sidehill, while others tend to roll over. The latter type may be excellent on the roads but disastrous on cross-country terrain and rough trails. If you run on rugged trails with unstable shoes, you are guaranteed a sprained ankle sooner or later.

During your first runs on rough trails, you will probably have a hard time picking out your steps, simply through lack of experience. Missteps are common, especially as you tire toward the end of a run. As the muscles that lift your legs become fatigued, you are also likely to trip. Try to pay particular attention to these factors, and keep your speed down when you aren't sure of yourself. Even as you get stronger, it is usually unwise to run at full speed on rugged downhills, except in race situations. Always maintain a good margin of safety when running trails. You will be able to do this at a faster pace as you gain experience on rough terrain. Be careful of overhanging branches when you are watching the trail. It is easy to be distracted by tricky footing and to injure an eye on a small branch hanging above the trail.

When you are racing on trails, footing can be a deciding factor on the hills. Getting good traction as you are driving up the hill while your opponent slips on mud or loose gravel can gain several feet and a precious bit of energy for you. Experience on the trails is the best guide here, since there are a thousand tiny judgments to be made on each hill: whether to use a little energy to jump forward slightly so as to catch hold of an imbedded rock for the next stride or to shorten your stride to avoid the mud just below; whether to duck under a branch or run around it. Most of these judgments have to become reflexive, and you can develop those reflexes only by running frequently on trails.

On trail runs, passing other runners is often a problem, and your whole strategy for a race may be based on your knowledge of a trail. In the famous Pike's Peak Marathon, for example, which is entered by a large field of runners, there is a short distance through the streets of town before the course starts up the Baird Trail. Since the trail is fairly narrow for some distance, making it very difficult to pass large numbers of runners, it is crucial to run fast enough in town to pass all the slower runners before you enter the trail bottleneck. Otherwise you will be forced to waste a lot of time and energy running up sidehills later on to get past them.

Traditionally, most trail races in the United States have been cross-country meets between schools at distances of two miles or a little more. But with the growth of distance running, there are more and more long trail races being organized all over the country, and many of them are run over classic courses. Competition can be stiff, but ordinary runners have a better chance of winning these races, because Olympic-class runners often stay away. Even if distances are certified, there is no chance of running a fast time on a rugged course compared to the same distance on a smooth surface. It is difficult and largely irrelevant to certify the length of such courses because of the uneven terrain, so the distances listed are usually unofficial. Such races are therefore usually left to those who are not fighting over national titles. Tactics and strategy also play a larger role, so cagey runners who gauge their own strength, the course, the weather, and the competition well can frequently make a good showing even against racers with much faster track times.

RACING TACTICS ON THE HILLS

Except on trail runs where footing, cornering, and passing situations complicate matters, tactics on the hills are essentially a more complex version of standard racing tactics. Because hills complicate a course and worry many racers, the challenge of pacing yourself becomes a bit more difficult. The opportunities for psyching out the competition are greater, and so are the dangers of becoming demoralized yourself. Pouring on the steam as you head up a hill wastes energy, but for this very reason it can be devastating to someone who is running even with you. Don't try to do it unless you are very sure of yourself.

If you do accelerate up a hill, don't look back at your opposition—the idea is to look as if you hardly even notice you're running up a hill at all. By looking back, you'll spoil the effect. If someone else uses this technique on you, it's usually best not to take the bait. Pace yourself up the hill at a good rate, keep the tempo at the top, and then use your downhill running technique on the other side to make up distance with a minimum of effort. Chances are that the hill will take its toll, and you'll catch your competitor either on the downhill side or later in the race. If the other person is really so much stronger that the hill doesn't faze him or her at all, you'll be even worse off if you burn out on the hill. If you decide to match the opposition stride for stride, remember that he or she is barely holding on, too. Stick with the pace setter and try to look as though there's nothing to it—then relax and pull ahead on the downside. Nothing is more demoralizing than trying to wipe someone out on a hill and failing.

CHAPTER VIII

BUILDING STRENGTH:

Resistance Training

ONE MAJOR TYPE of resistance work—hill running—was discussed in the previous chapter. Resistance training simply refers to those forms of exercise in which the muscle works against greater resistance than it encounters during normal activity. In the case of hill running, the resistance is the weight of the body; when you run hills, you not only have to project your weight in the series of coordinated jumps that constitute running but you're forced to move it up an incline as well. Different forms of resistance exercise can include other types of running that require more than average effort, nonrunning activities like bicycling that may require more effort from certain muscles than running does, and exercises like weight training designed solely for the purpose of building strength, power, or endurance in a particular group of muscles.

The whole subject of resistance training remains rather controversial. Some experts contend that a considerable amount of resistance work, often including formal weight training, is an important component of any balanced training program for

Sit-ups are a good traditional exercise, working both the stomach muscles and the hip flexors. I recommend bent-leg sit-ups to exercise the abdominal muscles, which tend to be weak in runners. (Regular sit-ups only work the abdominal muscles during the first part, after which the stress shifts to the hip flexors.) The first part of the sit-up (shown in illustration) can be repeated by itself if your stomach muscles are especially weak. You should do three sets in a session, with as many as you can do in each set—the important thing is to divide the exercise into three even efforts, with rests in between, rather than a single exhausting effort. To make the sit-ups easier, put your hands on your stomach; to make them harder, hold them above your head or hold a weight behind your neck.

The muscles in the lower back can be exercised by lying on your stomach and arching your back to pull both your legs and your upper trunk off the ground as high as you can. Try to keep your legs straight and to lift your head as far as possible. Then relax. Do three sets of this exercise in a session, repeating as many times as you can while maintaining the same number in each set. This exercise is easier with your arms at your sides, harder with your arms straight out in front of you.

One method of strengthening the upper hamstrings is to loop a bicycle inner tube over a tree branch or other high anchor, put your leg through, and pump vigorously up and down. Do three sets of this exercise five minutes apart, experimenting to see how many and how hard you can push and still complete all three sets. Do this exercise *after* running. Exercise your weaker leg first, and do the same number of repetitions with each leg. The lower hamstrings can be exercised easily, too, by looping the inner tube low down on the tree trunk, hooking your lower leg through, and pulling back. Tension is governed in this position by how high the inner tube is looped on the calf.

A better exercise for the lower hamstrings is to use weights, because the force is more constant. You can use a nylon sack containing several weights, but a sand or feed sack will work equally well. Stand with one leg behind you, and drape the weight sack over that heel. By bending the knee and raising the weight, you exercise the lower hamstrings. This exercise can also be used for the buttocks and upper hamstrings, by raising your leg straight in back of you, without bending the knee. Do as many as you can of each type, again divided into three even sets. Exercise the weaker leg first, and do an equal number of repetitions with each leg. A variation: By sitting on a chair or bench, looping the weight over the top of the foot and then straightening the leg out in front of you, the quadriceps are exercised with the same device.

A bicycle tube is also handy for exercising the lower leg, ankle, and foot. Hitch the inner tube on any solid object near the ground, hook the other end over your toe, and pull the toe back against the tension. This exercise strengthens the front muscles of the lower leg and helps to prevent shinsplints. Do three sets with each leg. Do this exercise *after* running.

From the same position, you can exercise the inner and outer muscles of the ankle and foot. With the inner tube hooked over your instep turn your foot inward against the resistance, adjusting the force by pulling back so that the inner tube is tighter at the beginning of the routine. Do three sets of ten repetitions each to exercise the inside muscles of the foot and ankle, and repeat equally with each foot. To exercise the outside muscles of foot and ankle, repeat this routine turning your foot *outward* against the resistance. These foot exercises help to prevent overuse injuries and sprained ankles.

the runner. The great Australian coach Percy Cerutty, who supervised the careers of champions like Herb Elliott and John Landy, was a strong believer in many forms of resistance exercise for proper running development. Cerutty's athletes ran in sand and water, sprinted up sand dunes, and did calisthenics, gymnastic exercises, and weight training for abdominal and upper-body strength.

Others argue that the best training for running is simply running, and that other forms of exercise are a waste of time, except in special circumstances, such as during an injury. They cite the principle of specificity, maintaining that nothing is more specific to running than going out on the roads and putting in the miles. Particularly with respect to upper-body exercises, they feel that any extra weight, including muscle weight, is waste baggage to the runner, and they note that many distance runners in long continuous training tend to become more efficient by losing weight in the upper body, from muscle tissue as well as extra fat.

Our present level of knowledge does not really give us any clear answers to the various arguments about resistance training, especially about weight training, except in a few specialized areas. This is particularly true for distance running, since the case for resistance training is easier to make for sprinters and hurdlers, who rely more on strength and power for rapid acceleration and all-out effort over a short period of time.

BALANCING MUSCULAR DEVELOPMENT

One area in which the case for some resistance exercise is clear is in balancing the strength of muscles in the legs. Many injuries can result from legs of unequal strength and from opposing muscles in either leg that are not balanced in their strength. But extensive distance running does not produce balanced development of the muscles, and the exaggerated strengthening of those muscles along the backs of the legs can result both in shortening and in muscle pulls. Thus, an excellent case can be made for compensatory training exercises to balance leg strength. A similar argument is made by weight-training advocates for some of the muscles of the upper body, like those in the upper back that counterbalance the chest muscles—during the later stages of long runs, they contend, fatigue in these muscles impedes proper breathing and posture.

Some specific exercises for those leg muscles that tend to be weak in distance runners are included in Chapter XIV, and the rest of this chapter will describe briefly some of the techniques that can be used by those who would like to try an overall resistance-training program. One thing that is certain, whether it helps your running or not, is that such a program will improve your overall fitness and is not likely to hurt your running. The real argument is whether serious competitive runners who have limited time and energy for training are using their time efficiently by doing resistance work.

MUSCLE STRENGTH

In training for strength, the athlete can have many different objectives, and it is important to have a fairly precise idea of the effects of different types of exercise and of your own objectives. What we actually mean by "strength" is often rather vague. It can mean the capacity to hold a heavy weight or lift it from one position to another, the ability to propel yourself or a heavy object with great force, or the faculty of continuing to do work for long periods of time. These are quite different muscular feats, though there is a continuum between them and no clear dividing line. Who is stronger: a person who can lift 250 pounds once, someone who can lift 175 pounds ten times, or someone who can lift 100 pounds fifty times? How about the speed with which they can perform each of these actions?

If you use weight training for building strength—and it is certainly one of the most versatile forms of resistance training—the principle of specificity of training applies. If you want to develop *absolute strength,* you should lift very heavy weights a few times. To accelerate a relatively heavy weight quickly, normally referred to as *power,* you should lift moderate weights rapidly a number of times. To develop *endurance,* you should lift light weights many times. Except for maximum weights, all these descriptions are relative, of course, as are the qualities they develop. The specific recommendations given later in the chapter will illustrate what they mean in practice.

Another important factor in strength is the range of motion over which it is developed. If you stress a muscle against heavy resistance in one position—a so-called *isometric* contraction— you will develop a great deal of strength in that position, but not in others. This type of training is generally undesirable for runners, both because it limits the application of the developed strength and because it is the type of exercise that decreases flexibility and may increase muscle bulk. Any training exercises done for strength should force the muscle to work over its full range of movement.

One myth about resistance-type exercises, especially weight training, is that they necessarily develop large muscle bulk, produce a muscle-bound condition, and reduce flexibility, range of movement, and agility. None of these effects necessarily accompany even intense weight training. A muscle-bound condition, like the inflexibility of some distance runners, is usually caused by heavy and imbalanced exercise. Increased muscle bulk results from a particular type of weight lifting, cultivated by body-building enthusiasts. Properly balanced weight training will leave the runner lean and probably more supple than before the strength program was begun.

CALISTHENICS

You can develop a good deal of upper-body strength and balance the muscles used heavily in running with calisthenics by using only body weight, though by using weights it is sometimes easier to isolate specific muscles. But the average runner can do a great deal of effective strength training without any special equipment at all. The main disadvantage of calisthenics

using only body weight is that you cannot progressively increase the resistance involved, so that they change more and
more into endurance-type exercises as you get stronger and do
more repetitions.

Many very useful basic exercises are well-known. Push-ups,
pull-ups, and dips develop the muscles of the arms, chest, and
upper back. (Dips involve lowering and then raising your body
weight with your arms, with supports on either side of your
body, and with your legs hanging free. Parallel bars are traditionally used for this exercise, but the backs of two chairs or
any other solid objects will do.) If you can't do many push-ups
at first in the traditional way, keep your knees resting on the
ground and push up only your upper body.

When combined with stretches, these calisthenics will improve your strength a good deal. Do them three times a week,
with rest days in between, and you will see a lot of improvement in your strength. Remember that several sets of each during a session are more effective than one push to exhaustion.
When these calisthenics become easy, you can decide whether
you want to work into weight training.

WEIGHT-TRAINING PRINCIPLES

The importance of doing lifts that require a full range of
motion has already been mentioned. Equally important to the
runner is a careful balancing of the exercises you do. Always do
the exercises for opposing groups of muscles in the same session. Strengthening one group while ignoring the opposing
group is asking for trouble, unless you are rectifying a pre-
viously existing imbalance. Similarly, if you use equipment or
routines that exercise the two sides of the body separately,
always use the same weights and the same number of repetitions, determined for the weaker side. There is a natural tendency to slack off as you proceed with any group of exercises,
so when there are natural separations, exercise the weak side or
the weak group of muscles first.

Lifting heavy weights can be dangerous if you are careless

about learning how to use them. A safe area clear of junk and with a nonslip floor is essential. Runners with any postural problems, particularly in their backs, should consult a physician before attempting any weight lifting. Exercises should be learned carefully with light weights before trying heavier ones. Beginners should never try lifting very heavy weights to the overhead position, as in competitive weight lifting. Such lifts require both good technique and strong back muscles. They have to be practiced over a period of time to be performed safely, and I don't recommend them for runners. Don't do any weight training when you are tired after a hard workout, and don't lift a heavier weight or accomplish a repetition by distorting the proper lifting position, especially by bending over backwards.

The recommended weights for particular exercises are given in terms of the maximum weight that you can lift in that position. Ascertain this weight carefully through experimentation, working up slowly over a period of several days if necessary. A universal weight machine, often available at municipal recreation centers or YMCAs, is ideal for the purpose, since it does not require handling heavy barbells or dumbbells.

Like push-ups, pull-ups, and dips, weights are useful for progressive development of strength, power, and endurance—especially so, because the resistance used can be easily controlled.

UPPER BODY EXERCISES

The Military Press: Standing up straight with your feet slightly apart, begin with the barbell resting on your chest. Press the barbell straight up over the head. For strength development, begin with a weight twenty pounds less than the maximum you can press in this position. Try to do three sets of five or six repetitions each, pressing fairly slowly. If this is not possible, you should reduce the weight. When you can easily do three sets of six, increase the weight by five pounds. For power development, use half the maximum weight you can press, and do three sets of a dozen repetitions each, pressing as rapidly and explosively as possible. Increase the weight by five pounds when this becomes easy. For endurance, press one quarter your maximum for two sets of about twenty-five repetitions each. Again, increase the weight by five pounds when the exercise becomes easy. A good variation that shifts the stress to the muscles further back in the shoulders is to begin with the barbell on the back of your neck and press straight up.

Rowing: Stand partially bent over, feet slightly apart, and grip the barbell with your hands about three feet apart. Bend your knees slightly and hang your arms (with barbell) straight down. The barbell should hang just below your knees. Lift the weight to your chest without moving the knees or body, and then lower it again. For strength development, begin with a weight fifteen pounds lighter than your maximum in this position, and do three sets of five repetitions, lifting slowly. Adjust the weight as with the military press. For power, use a weight half the maximum you can lift in this position and do three sets of twelve, lifting rapidly and explosively. For endurance, use one fifth your maximum and do two sets of twenty-five repetitions.

LOWER BODY EXERCISES

To strengthen the muscles of the lower back, hips, and hamstrings, place the bar behind your neck, bend over at the waist so that your body is at a right angle (no further), and straighten up again. Do three sets of five or six repetitions each, increasing the weight by five pounds when three sets of six become easy. This exercise can be dangerous if you start with too heavy a weight, so begin with a light weight and increase it gradually.

To strengthen the muscles of the upper legs and hips, the standard exercise is the squat. You should begin with a one-third squat: Stand straight with your heels slightly elevated (on a brick, or other block). Rest the barbell on the back of your neck. Then squat down, keeping the body as straight as possible, until your thighs and calves are at about a right angle to one another. The full squat, letting the backs of the thighs touch the calves, is safe if you do not bounce and you know your limits, but it requires care. Start with forty pounds under the maximum weight you can lift in this position, or work up slowly from a light weight until you know your limits. The block under the heel improves stability and safety. Do two sets of a dozen squats each.

An alternative to the squat that avoids the use of heavy weights and is therefore safer for beginners is the step-up, which exercises one leg at a time. Stand with one foot up on a low chair or other elevation that bends the leg at about a right angle (a step about knee-high). Holding the barbell at the back of the neck, step up, stand with both feet on the chair, and then step down again. Start this exercise with twenty pounds under the maximum weight you can handle and do two sets of six each. Be sure to lower yourself back to the ground slowly to exercise all the muscles.

The exercises described here require no special equipment except for a barbell and weights, and they are quite simple and safe for a person working alone. Other pieces of equipment— weight boots, dumbbells, a bench—are helpful if you find weight training worthwhile. For discussion of equipment and a more detailed consideration of all phases of weight training, the best book for the runner is John Jesse's *Strength, Power and Muscular Endurance for Runners and Hurdlers.*

CHAPTER IX

ALTITUDE TRAINING

THE EFFECTS OF altitude on performance can easily be seen by comparing the results of the 1968 Olympics with those of preceding and succeeding contests. The 5000-meter winning times in 1964 and 1972 were 13:48.8 and 13:26.4; in 1968 the race was won in 14:05.0. The 10,000-meter winners in 1964 and 1972 ran 28:24.4 and 27:38.4; in 1968 the winner ran 29:27.4. The 1964 and 1972 marathons were won in 2:12:11.2 and 2:12:19.8, while the 1968 event required 2:20:26.4. There is no mystery in the dramatically increased times; the 1968 Olympic games were held in Mexico City at an altitude of 2245 meters (7364 feet), where the pressure of oxygen is less, reducing the supply that is available to be extracted by the lungs and transmitted to the bloodstream and the muscles.

Perhaps even more interesting to the distance runner is the list of winners at the distance races in Mexico City. The Kenyans, raised and trained at high altitude, dominated the distance events overwhelmingly. Their great runners provided powerful competition before and after the Mexico games, but never dominated the games so exclusively in other years.

130

Altitude training has also been an important part of the regimens of a number of very strong distance runners, including marathon gold medalists Abebe Bikila, Mamo Wolde, and Frank Shorter; and so it is worth sorting out a few of the effects of altitude. Some are well understood, while others are speculative. From a practical point of view, there are also a number of distinct problems that runners may have to consider in connection with altitude changes, such as the question of when to travel to a race being held at a different altitude or the matter of balancing altitude training with other techniques.

ALTITUDE AND OXYGEN PRESSURE

During normal breathing at sea level, the blood passing through the lungs is intimately associated with the fresh air (or exhaust fumes!) that you have just inhaled. This air, under atmospheric pressure, is partially composed of oxygen. The pressure exerted by the oxygen on everything around it is called the partial pressure of oxygen. This partial pressure is a percentage of total atmospheric pressure. At sea level, this pressure is sufficient to saturate the blood with almost as much oxygen as it can hold. Hemoglobin, the oxygen-binding agent in the blood, becomes nearly saturated with oxygen each time it is circulated through the lungs. At higher altitudes, however, where both total atmospheric pressure and the partial pressure of oxygen are lower, hemoglobin is not able to bind as much oxygen. As a consquence, the red blood cells are not able to transport as much oxygen.

At higher elevations, therefore, each red cell in the blood is able to carry less oxygen to the working muscles of the body as it moves through the circulatory system, so that less oxygen is obtained from each breath taken in by the lungs, from each stroke of the heart, or from each unit of blood pumped through a muscle. At moderate elevations, this fact has little impact on a healthy person at rest or engaged in moderate activity. The heart may have to pump a little more rapidly, the lungs may have to be inflated a little more often; but since we have so much reserve capacity in all the body functions that affect oxygen supply, the difference is made up without our really noticing it.

The picture is quite different in situations when the body would normally have to work hard to supply adequate oxygen. Thus, people with respiratory or circulatory disorders can be affected by even moderate altitude gains, and so can athletes or other individuals working at a high level of oxygen uptake. Runners are affected to some degree at altitudes that do not affect the daily routines of individuals in normal health.

There is a tremendous number of problems involved with the effects of altitude, all of them complex and incompletely understood. Only those that most directly affect the runner will be discussed here. The extreme difficulties of acclimatization that affect the high-altitude mountaineer will scarcely be touched on, for example, because the runner does not experience extreme altitude. Most races are held below 8000 feet, and even the highest mountain races in the United States ascend to only a little over 14,000 feet for a brief period. Long-range altitude effects are not felt in this short time. A foot ascent also eliminates many of the acute effects of altitude sometimes experienced in connection with air travel.

A little over a fifth of the air we breathe consists of oxygen. At elevations below those of the highest mountains, both atmospheric and oxygen pressure decrease at a relatively constant rate for each thousand meters of altitude gained. The pressure at an altitude of 2000 meters (6562 feet) will be about 88 percent of the pressure at 1000 meters (3281 feet), and the pressure at 3000 meters (9843 feet) will be about 88 percent of the pressure at 2000 meters.

The reduction in the ability of the blood to transport oxygen does not occur at this constant rate, however. An increase in altitude from sea level to 4000 meters (13,124 feet) produces an effect much greater than double that of an increase from sea level of 2000 meters (6562 feet). The effects are almost negligible up to an elevation of 1000 meters (3281 feet). They begin to increase more quickly above 1500 meters (4921 feet) or so, and they rise dramatically above 3000 meters (9843 feet).

This reduced capacity of the blood to carry oxygen has profound consequences for the runner at high altitude. At 3500 meters above sea level (11,482 feet) each red blood cell is capable of binding only about 90 percent of its maximum oxygen capacity, whereas at sea level it will reach almost full saturation each time it passes through the lungs. The reduced quantity of oxygen that can be carried by the blood has to be compensated for in other ways to maintain performance. For distance runners who are already performing at the highest levels they can sustain during a long race, decreased performance is inevitable.

ACCLIMATIZATION

If you stay at high altitude for some time, your body will make a number of changes to deal with the reduced oxygen pressure. Not all these changes are fully understood, and they are difficult to study since some apparently take place at the cellular level in the working muscles. The adaptations take place at different rates, and these changes are not quite the same for a person living at sea level who moves to altitude as for the native who lives at high elevations from birth. Some changes begin to reverse themselves when a person descends to sea level, while others apparently do not. There are complicated side effects beyond the simple relationship between reduced oxygen pressure and consequent deterioration in performance. For example, digestion may be impeded by the reduction in oxygen supply, particularly if you eat fatty foods while doing heavy exercise. Heavy breathing causes increased exhalation of carbon dioxide, which in turn affects the acidity of the blood and the fluid around the brain and spinal cord. Changes in carbon dioxide concentration affect breathing, particularly during sleep, and erratic breathing can disturb rest. It is obvious to any runner that performance can be impaired by poor sleep and digestive disruptions. Complicating matters still further, people acclimatize at very different rates, so that the figures given here are averages. Some individuals are also particularly susceptible to the unpleasant side effects of acclimatization like headache and upset stomach.

The first effect of altitude on the body is a reduction of its capacity for maximum oxygen consumption, for the reasons already noted. This capacity continues to decline for the next day or two. It follows that if you live at sea level and are planning to run a high-altitude race, you should either allow a fair amount of time for acclimatization or you should plan on arriving just before the race. Spending a day or two at altitude before the race is likely to bring you to your lowest point in performance. On exposure to altitude, the heart and lungs begin to work harder to compensate for reduced oxygen pressure. The first real adaptation in the oxygen supply system, however, seems to be a reduction in blood volume. Essentially, the body increases the concentration of oxygen-carrying red cells by reducing the liquid content of the blood. Over the long run, additional cells are produced and the red blood cell count is increased, but it takes weeks for this increased production to make a significant difference and about a year before it is complete. This may be one of the advantages of long-term training at high altitude, but this question is discussed in more detail later in the chapter.

Other short-term adaptations include changes in sensitivity to carbon dioxide concentration in the blood and the cerebrospinal fluid. It is these changes that eliminate the difficulties in sleeping experienced by many lowlanders when they first come to altitude. Other chemical changes occur that are not fully understood. Performance begins improving again after the first two days of exposure and continues to get better, at first rapidly and then more and more slowly. Basic adaptation is complete after two to three weeks. Longer-term adaptation continues for years and includes better circulation in the brain and the working muscles. Apparently the gradual increase in the volume of red cells in the blood is accompanied by a slow increase in the diameter and number of blood vessels in the working muscles and nervous system which permits a larger volume of red cells through. Thus, natives living and working hard at altitudes as high as 4000 meters (13,124 feet) have been reported to be able to process as much oxygen as young athletic men at sea level. (Some specific references are mentioned in the bibliography at the end of the book.)

From a practical point of view, there are several acclimatization questions that arise for runners competing at various altitudes: What are the best procedures for a lowlander competing at altitude? How much faster should a person living at high altitude plan on running a sea-level race? And finally, what are the advantages and best techniques for altitude training, both for specific races at altitude and for long-term conditioning?

RACING AT HIGH ALTITUDE

There is probably no practical way for the lowland native to make up for the advantage of a person living at high altitude for some kinds of distance races, as shown by the results at the Mexico City Olympics. On the other hand, the difficulty of competing in such races is not nearly as great as many runners have come to believe. Lowland natives seem to be at no disadvantage at all at elevations up to 2000 meters or so (6562 feet). The 15-kilometer Run for the Roses in Boulder, Colorado, in 1978—over a mile above sea level—was won by Minnesotan Gary Bjorklund, with Mike Slack of Chicago taking second place, despite a star-studded field of runners living in the area, including Olympian Frank Shorter and record holder Ric Rojas. Even a race as specialized as the uphill half of the Pikes Peak Marathon, which involves a climb of nearly 8000 feet (2438 meters) to the summit of a mountain 14,110 feet (4301 meters) high, has been won by David Castillas, a resident of Illinois.

If your race is not serious enough to warrant your spending a week or more at altitude, the best strategy is probably to arrive a few hours before the race, or as close to race time as possible. If you plan to eat before the race, avoid fatty foods, which are harder to digest than carbohydrates; this should fit well with a competitor's normal racing diet, anyway. If you are spending the previous night at altitude, be sure to arrive well rested as insurance in case you have trouble sleeping. If you suffer from a headache after arriving at altitude, you should take aspirin or some other mild headache remedy, since there is a tendency for altitude headaches to get worse and contribute to nausea.

If you are training at altitude for a week or more prior to the race, it is usually best to get out and start running hard as soon as possible, since a workout helps to stimulate the process of acclimatization. But if you're staying above 3000 meters (about 10,000 feet), you may do well to make an exception, since high-altitude pulmonary and cerebral edema can occur at this elevation, and these are potentially fatal disorders; it's a good idea to postpone your first workout for twenty-four hours at this altitude.

You should probably run your first workout at race pace, so that you immediately start to develop a feel for the effect of the altitude. In distance events, above an elevation of 1500 meters (4921 feet) you will probably find that running at normal effort will result in a slightly slower pace than at sea level. Your kick will be just as fast as at lower altitude, presumably because the anaerobic metabolism is not significantly affected by the altitude. However, your recovery from a speed burst or a hard hill climb will be much slower than it is at home. The cost of going into oxygen debt in a race is much greater, so that careful pacing is more critical at a high-altitude race than at home, particularly for the runner who has had little experience at elevations much above sea level.

You may have little trouble adjusting to the altitude, but you should be mentally prepared for some initial discomfort and for declining performance through your first few days. The usual speed-work sessions, tapering off for the race, should be used for training, depending on the time you have available. But you should also concentrate on refining your pacing, especially if the race is high enough so that it will be run at a significantly slower speed than you are used to. Your pacing sense is likely to be thrown off, particularly above 2000 meters (6562 feet), because the demand on your lungs will be greater for a particular leg speed. Some runners are thrown off more than others, because some gauge their pacing mainly from oxygen demand while others concentrate on leg rhythm. Be careful in your race tactics, particularly against local runners, who will have a better feel for how hard they can push. When you're not used to the elevation for a high-altitude race, the best strategy is an evenly paced one with a kick at the end. Beware of starting your kick too soon, since you will go into oxygen debt more quickly, but don't hold back as you near the finish. Plan your race carefully and stick to the plan. In long races be sure to get enough liquid. Dehydration can be a problem because of dry air and reduced blood volume.

TRAINING AT HIGH ALTITUDE

There are several potential advantages to training at altitude besides preparation for specific races. Because a large demand on the lungs and circulatory system is produced by a slower pace than at sea level, training at altitude is an excellent way to develop great efficiency in delivering oxygen to the muscles. For good runners doing base training, running at high altitude is superb conditioning. Many good runners who are not in the elite category have found that a period of altitude training gives excellent results.

It is important to note, however, that training at altitude is no panacea and even has a few drawbacks. Since oxygen delivery is not the limiting factor in the performance of World-class runners, maximum oxygen consumption per unit of body weight does not determine who will do best in a race. Oxygen delivery is often a determinant for less talented or less well-trained runners, but elite runners have developed enough oxygen-processing capacity to bring them up to other performance limits.

The sea-level records of athletes who live and train regularly at high altitude seem to bear out this observation. Though altitude training has obviously been useful in their training, they are not superior to runners from sea level except in high-altitude races. Thus, altitude training should be regarded as an excellent tool, like intervals or hill training, but hardly an indispensable one.

The opportunity to train at high elevations is likely to come to most runners in connection with other activities, so a training area is rarely chosen solely on the basis of its height above sea level. Any training at altitudes of 1500 meters (4921 feet) or higher is bound to have some benefit. Basically, the higher the elevation, the more cardiopulmonary training stimulus there will be. At the same time, your speed will be affected in inverse proportion, because you will not be running as fast. High elevations are not particularly good for sharpening because of the generally slower pace you will manage at any given level of effort. Runners training at altitude and trying to sharpen for racing have to counteract this problem with a good deal of interval and *fartlek* work using short distances.

At elevations of around 1500 meters (4921 feet) the runner's speed will be affected only slightly, and training should proceed just as it would at sea level, though times in long races and speed sessions will be a little slower. Runners working at altitudes very much above 2000 meters (6562 feet) will be slowed significantly and will have a difficult time sharpening to maximum speed. This has no disadvantage for the recreational runner, but the serious racer has to take it into consideration. Racers living near 3000 meters (9843 feet) will find it virtually impossible to develop full leg speed without doing some speed work at lower altitude.

An ideal use of altitude training would be to run the last couple of months of base training at an elevation of 2000 meters (6562 feet), with some hill-training runs that add another thousand meters, followed by sharpening and speed training at sea level. But since few of us plan our lives around our running, we aren't likely to have the opportunity of regulating things so neatly. A vacation in the mountains can provide the dedicated runner with a nice opportunity of trying some running at high altitude, and it may help in sea-level races later on.

CHAPTER X

UPPING THE PACE

THERE IS NOTHING at all wrong with running races directly from your base training, instead of sharpening with speed work, and many recreational runners will want to do just that. The closer you get to your maximum capacity for speed, the more unnatural strain you will put on your body in the process. Continuing your base training and running an occasional race—how many should depend on your training, the effort you put into them, and on the distances involved—is a pleasant way to sample some of the excitement of racing without becoming obsessed. Moreover, if you still have not become really fit during base training, you may be much better off by not sharpening. If you are still well over racing weight, for example, you shouldn't do a lot of speed work. Stick with base-training methods and fun races until you have trimmed down. Losing weight is the most effective way for you to speed up, anyway. Remember that you trim four or five seconds off your time in each mile of a race for every couple of pounds you trim off your stomach.

If exploring your own limits is one of the major satisfactions that you get from running, however, you are likely to want to see just how fast you can run some of the time. Sharpening and peaking are crucial phases in training to run fast. They exploit the capital you have built up in base training and develop it, building speed onto the foundation of aerobic training that you have laid down over the preceding months.

LEARNING TO RUN FAST

The virtues of running at a moderate pace have been extolled through much of this book, but there is no question that in order to run fast in a race you have to run fast in training. Training at relatively slow speeds and sticking primarily to aerobic running can take you only so far. Fast running requires that the muscles learn to coordinate at higher speeds, recruiting the necessary motor units in the acting muscles and completely relaxing the inactive ones at each instant of the stride. All this has to be done with as little tension and extraneous effort in the body as possible, otherwise fatigue builds up and slows you down sooner than necessary. You have to raise your aerobic limits further and develop a tolerance for anaerobic effort, learning just how far you can go into oxygen debt at any point in a run without sustaining an overall loss.

The sharpening phase of training can accomplish all of these purposes, developing your speed and bringing you to peak form for a period of six weeks or a few months. At the same time, you make longer-term progress in developing your running times and experience, so that you will be able to start building from a higher level of base performance during your next sharpening period.

During all phases of sharpening, you should remember that there are several elements to developing speed. One is pushing yourself. If you have a background of high school or college track or other experience of hard, competitive running, you will already have a feeling for the effort of all-out running. If you began with aerobic distance running and have never done any serious speed work or racing before, you may not really know the feeling of really pushing, however. The hard days of the sharpening period are just that—hard. You have to spread your effort over an entire hill workout or set of intervals, but you should be pretty spent by the end of the session, especially during the first few weeks while you are getting used to the work load. If an interval session or a hard hill workout is to do any good, you can't finish it feeling as though you had just done an easy ten-mile run in the country. You shouldn't take three days to recover from an interval workout, but you shouldn't finish it feeling fresh, either. For aerobic runners, the first few anaerobic sessions are likely to be agony. It is hard to judge just how hard to push at first—you don't yet know how hard you *can* push. The only way to find out is really to extend yourself at first, until you have some idea how a tough workout should feel.

Experienced runners who have done fast intervals before shouldn't go all out during the first few weeks of sharpening; they need to put in serious work, but should allow a few weeks before running at a maximum effort. Beginners at speed work, though, need at least a couple of real pushes right at the start to develop a feeling for the meaning of various levels of effort. Novices should revert to the same pattern as veterans after a couple of tough workouts.

Working hard is only half the battle of sharpening. The more difficult half is relaxing. Relaxing when you are running fast is the most critical element in developing good speed, and it is the most difficult to learn. Even in the 100-yard dash, the runner is fighting with fatigue during the last part of the race, and the winner is often the sprinter who can relax through the last 25 yards and avoid tying up and slowing down. The longer the race, the truer this is. Throughout speed training it is important to focus on running faster and on relaxing while you are doing so. This requires constant attention and concentration. Top distance runners do not look at the scenery or have much conversation during a race or a speed session. They fix their minds on their pace, the reactions of their bodies, and the maintenance of a relaxed stride. When you lose concentration, you start to tie up and you fatigue more rapidly.

TECHNIQUES OF SHARPENING

The fundamental element in any sharpening program is the introduction of fast running to develop the neuromuscular coordination and mental discipline that are essential to speed. Most of this fast training is done over relatively short distances to permit you to run a greater overall volume of really fast work by allowing waste products to be flushed out between spurts. There are a number of ways to arrange and combine these fast runs, but finding the right mixture and timing for optimum sharpening is quite tricky. Whereas almost any base training program will work as long as it includes enough volume without overstressing the runner, speed work has to be timed correctly to get good results. If you run too fast too soon, you are likely to burn out long before reaching maximum speed. Too slow a buildup will not be completely effective, either. Individuals peak at different rates, so the most effective sharpening can be done when you have some experience of the way your own body works. In general, those who are naturally quite fast tend to peak a little more quickly than those with less native ability. Speed work takes one or two months to bring on maximum sharpening, with six weeks about average.

Lydiard recommends a period of intensive hill training for a period of six weeks before beginning speed work. If you have been running some hills during base training, a month of sharpening work on the hills should be plenty. The techniques involved are discussed below. The purpose is to serve as a final toughening and strengthening period before speed work. Many coaches and runners don't use this kind of hill training and proceed instead directly into intervals or other speed work.

Intervals are the most common type of speed work, because of the discipline and control that they automatically entail. There are many runners, however, who do their sharpening without any formal intervals at all. One reason is that it is so easy to burn out during interval training. *Fartlek* can be used

quite effectively as a substitute by those with enough background, but for inexperienced racers I think that some interval
and pace work is important to develop the practice necessary
for effective pacing in races. One of the best forms of *fartlek* is
gradual acceleration during a long run to a very quick pace,
concentrating on smooth style and relaxation all the time, and
then a gradual reduction to a comfortable pace again. Some of
this surging has already been recommended during base training, but on a modest scale. During sharpening you should work
up to a fast, anaerobic pace, maintain it for anywhere from a
hundred yards to a half-mile, and then drop back gradually to
a comfortable pace.

In general, until you have gained enough experience to
make your own modifications in your sharpening schedule, you
should plan on doing about six weeks of speed work before
reaching your peak. Unless you are a beginner at fast running
just learning to push yourself after going into oxygen debt, you
should not try to force your speed too rapidly. Start your speed
work with surging or with *fartlek,* or do track intervals without
timing yourself for the first two weeks. Your times will be lousy
anyway, and starting off on the clock will only disappoint you
or tempt you to push too hard. Start off with longish distances,
440's or longer. If you are inclined to push yourself too hard,
you can keep from overdoing it by making the rest jogs between the hard runs short. The same idea applies when you are
running your speed work on the roads—increase your speed
for distances in excess of a quarter-mile to start off. After a
couple of weeks, mix in some longer stretches and time trials.
By this time you should have developed both leg speed and endurance at faster paces. Then begin working in some short
surges and sprints to bring your speed up still further.

WARMING UP, COOLING DOWN, AND STRETCHING

Many runners don't bother to either warm up or cool down
during base training. If you simply start running at a reasonable pace when training over longer distances at modest

speeds, you aren't likely to have problems, unless you are fighting off an injury or require a particularly slow start. Such habits can get you into trouble when you begin sharpening, however. It is important to stretch and to jog or run slowly so that the muscles become limber before you start a speed workout. You are far more likely to pull a muscle or develop tendon problems if you neglect this precaution. It is usually best to jog two or three miles before a hard speed workout.

Jogging or running slowly after a speed session is not quite so critical, but your muscles will recover a lot more quickly and ache less if you do. Easy running or walking after a hard workout maintains good blood circulation in the working muscles, so that the waste products that accumulate during the fast running have time to dissipate.

During base training it isn't terribly important for most runners whether stretching is done before and after running, or at some other time of day. (Obviously, if you are very tight or having problems with an injury, you should stretch a number of times a day, especially before and after running.) During sharpening the muscles are under particular stress, and they need all the protection you can give them. You should therefore at least stretch the leg muscles at the beginning and end of a workout. It is often helpful to do a few stretches in the middle of a session, too, if you start to feel tense or tight. Stretching is also helpful in ridding muscles of waste products after a hard training session. A recommended set of stretches is shown in Chapter XIV.

HILL TRAINING

If you have had a proper buildup of endurance during base training, a month of intense hill workouts provides a very useful starting phase for the sharpening period. Hill training is not absolutely essential and should probably be avoided by runners whose base training has insufficient depth. If you are working toward your first racing season, for example, and your training pace has only reached 8-minute miles or slower, really hard hill work would probably only deplete your reserves. You should try to run some hills several days a week during your last month of base training, but don't do a lot of heavy training on them. Runners who have just gotten over injuries that might be exacerbated by hill running (see Chapter VII) should also skip this phase. (Those who are still fighting injuries or who are run down should not be sharpening at all.)

But for the serious runner who has been training steadily at 60 miles a week or more and whose aerobic pace on full-length training runs is frequently well below 8-minute miles, I think that a month of hill training is good preparation for sharpening. I recommend that you do three solid hill sessions a week, with long, easy runs on the days in between, still taking one run a week of double your standard length—in the range of 20–30 miles, depending on your weekly mileage. The hill training sessions, if they are intense enough, are likely to be shorter than your usual runs, so your weekly mileage should drop a little during this period.

Techniques for hill training during this phase have already been outlined in Chapter VII, so they will not be detailed here. Lydiard-style training is one method: bounding up a hill with short, bouncing steps, running down fast, and striding out away from the hill before jogging back and repeating the exercise. Ron Dawes recommends the same routine, except that he runs up the hills hard instead of bounding. My own preference is to run a hilly trail hard, attacking the uphills, running the downhills at maximum pace, and concentrating on a fast but relaxed pace on the flats between. Whichever method you use, you should be working on leg speed and efficient technique on the downgrades and pushing hard on the uphills. This is oxygen-debt training and also functions to strengthen and toughen the legs. It should significantly improve your downhill speed and prepare you for speed work. You'll probably feel weaker after one or two weeks of hill work than you did at the start, but after three weeks or so you should start to feel powerful while sprinting up the hills.

A week's schedule during this period for someone who has been regularly running 100 miles per week in base training might look like this:

Sunday	Monday	Tuesday	Wednesday
25 miles on roads, moderate pace	Hill training session: 2-mile warm-up jog, 6 miles hard on hills, 2-mile cool-down jog	10 miles easy on roads	Hill training session: same as Monday

Thursday	Friday	Saturday
10 miles easy on roads	Hill training session	10 miles easy on roads

The hill training sessions in the schedule above might consist of six hard miles on a trail with very steep hills or could be done on a single hill. For example, with a quarter-mile hill: Run hard up the hill; turn and run down it fast without pausing, striving for relaxation and high speed; continue striding out from the hill at a good pace a quarter-mile; jog back to the base of the hill; repeat the sequence five more times.

Note that the weekly mileage in the example has dropped from 100 miles a week to 85. As you increase the "quality" or intensity of the running you are doing, you should reduce the distance load somewhat. Battling to maintain your mileage as you move into hill training and speed work is a mistake. In general this schedule should be stiffened or relaxed proportionally to the mileage you have been training on a regular basis. If you have been running 75 miles a week, the mileages in the schedule should all be reduced by a quarter; if you have been doing 125, they should be a fifth higher than the ones shown. Two daily runs can be used instead of one, but the overall mileage should come down as intensity goes up.

SPEED WORK

Following this period of intensive hill training, it is time to begin building your speed proper. Again, I feel that three hard sessions a week is about the right number. More is certainly too many; some runners are better off doing only two. The speed sessions can be substituted for the hill workouts in the preceding schedule. As I indicated in the earlier introductory sections, you can build up your speed successfully with a number of types of workout—intervals, *fartlek*, or surging. The choice should be governed by your own feelings and perhaps by an analysis of your temperament. If you tend to slack off too much when you should be doing intense training, you should probably force yourself to do intervals—it's harder to cheat. If, on the other hand, you are so competitive that you end up racing instead of training when you get on the track, you might be better off sticking to *fartlek* and surging most of the time.

For most distance runners, I think that this is the time to do interval work a couple of days a week. A *fartlek* session for the midweek speed session will keep you from overdoing things on the track. Because this is a sharpening period, the formal and hard-working structure of a real interval workout is useful for most runners. The exact makeup of the workout will depend on the weekly mileage you are used to, but during the first couple of weeks you should concentrate on doing a lot of intervals in the longer-distance range with relatively short rests in between. Don't time them. During these first two weeks you should take advantage of the endurance capacity you have built up. At the beginning of the third week of the six-week sharpening period, start to time your intervals and take longer rest jogs in between the hard laps so that you can run them faster. In the last two weeks, as your speed improves, concentrate on shorter, faster sprints, building your leg speed to a maximum.

Some examples of routines for our hypothetical 100-mile-per-week runner should serve as an illustration of the principles involved. During the first two weeks, possible interval sessions would be:

2-mile warm-up jog; 4×440, 220 jog; 4×660, 220 jog; 4×880, 440 jog; 4×660, 220 jog; 4×440, 220 jog; 1-mile cool-down jog.

That is, you start out jogging a couple of miles (perhaps at an 8-minute-per-mile pace, if you train at around 7). You then run fast around a quarter-mile track four times, with each high speed run followed by a jog halfway around the track. Then take four hard runs lasting one and a half laps, interspersed with half-lap jogs; then four two-lap runs, followed by full-lap jogs; and so on. It may take a couple of sessions to learn the proper effort if you haven't run intervals before. Each sprint should take you far into oxygen debt, but you should recover during the subsequent jog. If you finish the whole session feeling at all fresh, you've been sloughing off. If you can't raise any effort during the second half of the workout, you're running the first part a little too hard. If you find that you are stiff and washed out for several days after a session, you're pushing the workout too much.

The entire session outlined above covers 13 miles, including the intervening jogs and the warm-up and cool-down runs. A runner who has been doing less than 100 miles a week should probably knock off a couple of the sprints, while one who has been doing more should add a couple of 1320's and a fast mile in the middle of the workout. The intervals listed earlier might be worked into an overall weekly schedule like this:

Sunday	Monday	Tuesday	Wednesday
25 miles on roads, moderate pace	Interval session, 13 miles	8 miles, easy, on roads	10 miles, stiff *fartlek* on trails

Thursday	Friday	Saturday
8 miles, easy, on roads	Interval session, 13 miles	8 miles, easy, on roads

Again, this works out to an 85-mile total for the week for someone who has been going 100 miles in base training. Others should adjust the mileage up or down accordingly.

The same interval routine could be used during the third week of speed training, when you begin timing your runs and pushing harder for speed; but the rest of the jogs should either be changed to walks or doubled in distance in order to increase recovery time and allow you to sprint faster.

During the fourth week you should start running shorter distances, pushing your speed up still more, and during the fifth and sixth weeks you should continue in this direction, reducing the volume of work somewhat, so that you can run faster. Some possible routines for the 100-mile-a-week runner would be:

Fourth week: 2 mile warm-up jog; 10×220, 220 jog; 10×440, 440 jog; 10×220, 220 jog; 1-mile cool-down jog.
Fifth and sixth weeks: 2-mile warm-up jog; 10×110, 220 jog; 5×220, 220 jog; 4×440, 440 jog; 5×220, 220 jog; 10×110, 220 jog; 1-mile cool-down jog.

Many runners have a hard time driving themselves out onto the track (or anywhere else) to do speed work. Intervals aren't much fun for a lot of us, even if we want to do the fast racing that they facilitate. For some of us, it's easy to make excuses and go on a long road run instead. Running with other people who have the same objectives is often helpful during the interval phase of your training, even if you normally train alone. There is the slight spur of competition to use when you want it. Be careful not to turn interval workouts into races, though. Don't run to "beat" someone or to show off. You should plan the workout you need and run it, using the other participants for support, not rivalry. Aim your peaks toward the races for which you are training, not toward some misguided challenge to your ego. The person who is fastest at the early stages of sharpening often fades by the time of the race.

TIME TRIALS

During the last half of the sharpening period, it is a good idea to run occasional time trials, so that you can begin working toward races and judge your progress. Local races make excellent occasions for this purpose, provided you can hold yourself back just a little. Time trials should be run hard but shouldn't drain your reserves badly. This is why some prefer to run them alone—you can never really go as hard running by yourself as you can in a race. For most people, though, low-key races make perfect time trials. Don't run anything longer than ten miles or so. Save the longer distances for serious racing.

You will have to modify your schedule somewhat to work local races into your training schedule, depending on when they occur. If there are usually Saturday-morning fun races scheduled in your area, for instance, you might drop your *fartlek* session, switch your interval workouts to Tuesday and Thursday, and run easy days on Monday, Wednesday, and Friday. Try doing a mile of tempo work in the middle of the Friday run, going at exactly the speed you plan to use on the longer race the following day. Run the rest of the Friday run at a very relaxed pace.

If everything goes according to schedule, you should be acquiring good speed by the end of the six-week sharpening period. By paying attention to the way you feel, you can make adjustments according to how well you are running, pointing the way toward whatever races or other runs you are preparing for. As you finish the peaking period, you should taper off your hard interval work, moving back over to relaxed running to retain your muscle tone and conditioning and doing some pace work and surging within your long runs to maintain speed and learn the pacing for particular races.

CHAPTER XI

EATING
AND RUNNING:

Basic Nutritional Principles

PEOPLE WHO ARE extremely fit naturally become more sensitive than the average individual to the effects of diet on their bodies. Such preoccupation can be healthy, though some runners become so obsessed with diet that they lose their sense of perspective. A lot more is written about the principles of nutrition and diet than is actually known, and a lot of the known facts have been fairly widely disseminated. Every schoolchild knows that adequate vitamins are important. Plenty of misinformation has been spread about, too, but much of it can be disposed of fairly quickly.

Many of the open questions on diet have more to do with long-term health than with running performance. Once the myths are dispelled, many dietary questions have more to do with your other attitudes about life than they do with your running. You can run just as well with a properly balanced vegetarian diet as with a conventional American diet. The hoary myth that athletes require steaks to build muscles is nonsense. On the other hand, except for making weight control easier, a

151

vegetarian diet will not make you run faster. It may improve your general health, especially over the long run, and it may make you feel better. But there are enough top runners around who indulge in standard junk-food diets to make it difficult to present a good case for the miraculous effects of diet on performance.

BODY WEIGHT, FAT, AND CALORIC INTAKE

One absolute correspondence between diet and performance is between caloric intake and body weight. There are some complicated side issues concerning why some people put on weight so much more easily than others. The generation of fat cells in the growing child has a strong influence on the eating patterns of the adult; many people are less compulsive about eating than others; some are naturally more active; and it may be that some people pass more food through the digestive system without extracting all the usable calories. It is definitely true that some people can eat more than others without gaining weight, even though their activity levels are apparently similar.

Basically, however, the equations are extremely simple. If you eat more calories than you burn, you will put on weight in the form of stored fat. If you burn more than you eat, you will lose weight. And if the two balance out, you will remain at a stable weight. These formulas hold true whether you are running fifteen miles a day or sitting in front of the TV. Another assertion that can be made with equal confidence is that light runners go faster and farther than heavy runners, given equivalent training.

Not all weight on the body is equal, however, either in cosmetic terms or in terms of health and performance. Muscle tissue is a good deal denser than fat, so that turning fat to muscle will make you look slimmer as well as make you fitter and healthier. Efficient runners have lean, tough muscle rather than bulging biceps, however, and experienced runners aren't likely to gain much muscle bulk unless they do heavy weight training. Athletes who train for absolute strength can be quite heavy while retaining a very low percentage of body fat. The extreme examples are male body builders. Whatever its other virtues, such muscle bulk is not helpful in distance running.

Most variations in weight between people of the same sex and height are due to body fat. The weight differences between people with heavy bones and those with light ones are quite small, in the range of a few pounds. There are a lot of sophisticated tests used to determine the exact amount of body fat in individuals, using scales that weigh the difference between dry weight and weight under water, but it is easy enough to tell whether you have extra fat without any fancy instruments. Any folds you can grab around your waist, hips, thighs, back, and upper arms are fat if they are more than about an eighth-inch thick and won't bulge up when you tense the local muscles. The amount of extra fat even on many fairly fit runners is amazing.

It stands to reason, though, that if you have any significant extra weight on your body and are trying to improve your performance, the most effective way to do it is to lose that weight. Running is a help in controlling weight, because it burns up quite a few calories and often serves as an appetite suppressant. Its effects are slow, however, and it cannot be considered a panacea. The figures vary somewhat with body weight and pace, but a typical adult will burn about 100 calories for each mile run. This can be a tremendous help over a period of a year—365,000 calories at ten miles a day—but it will not make any rapid inroads on the spare tire you are sporting from overindulgence through the winter. The best answer to weight problems for the serious runner is obviously to keep caloric intake in line with energy expenditures. You can't expect to lose weight very rapidly with a buildup in mileage alone; limiting your food intake and at the same time increasing your training is the only way to lose weight very quickly.

The various approaches open to the runner trying to lose weight rapidly are not much different from those open to anyone else. You can restrict your intake of food in a modest way—perhaps the healthiest approach and the slowest. By emphasizing fruits, vegetables, and whole grains in your diet and restricting your intake of fats and refined sugar, you can probably tip the balance and start losing weight fairly rapidly while still getting plenty of nutrients. If you want quicker weight loss, you will have to cut your food intake to a lower level; but make sure you are getting enough vitamins, minerals, and other essentials if you are training hard. Fasting is the quickest way to lose weight and is discussed in Chapter XIII.

Any diet that promotes very rapid weight loss, whether through fasting or very low caloric input, is likely to cause some loss of muscle tissue as well as of surplus fat. This is one reason why alternating crash diets and weight gains is so bad for inactive people. Some muscle tissue is lost during each diet, but most of the weight regained is in the form of fat. Runners are not likely to go through this cycle, since a runner in training doesn't put on very much weight. There is also some evidence that exercise during a diet or fast reduces the loss of muscle tissue—that is, the body seems to conserve the working tissues and concentrate the weight loss better into the fat stores. It is worth remembering, however, that staying slim is always healthier than having to lose large amounts of fat.

CARBOHYDRATES, FATS, AND PROTEINS

The most fundamental nutritional requirement of the body other than water to maintain adequate hydration and salt concentrations is fuel to burn for energy. The energy to run, or simply to sustain life, is provided by chemical reactions that amount to a controlled burning of fuel—combining it with oxygen and utilizing the energy released. The body has elaborate means of storing fuel so that it can function when you are not eating. Some of these are designed mainly for short-term use, while others are intended to sustain the body for long periods when food is lacking or inadequate. Since we are descended

from hunters and gatherers who often had to live without food
for some time, the body stores any extra food eaten in the form
of fat deposits that can later be reclaimed. In the present-day
United States there is a lot of storing but very little reclaiming.

Most of our food falls into three general classifications: carbohydrates, fats, and proteins. The majority of cells and organs
in the body function most easily when fueled with carbohydrates—sugars and starches. Carbohydrate metabolism is preferred by the runner because less oxygen is required to extract
energy from carbohydrates than from fats, the other major
source of fuel. Fats are important as fuel for several reasons,
which will be discussed more thoroughly later. Proteins can also
be used as fuel, but they are not used very efficiently by the
body for that purpose. They are a crucial part of the diet because they are necessary for the manufacture of new tissue.
They are therefore required for normal replacement of old
cells, for building up new muscle tissue under the stimulus of
training, and for the healing of any injuries. This fact was the
basis for speculation in the past that athletes needed large
amounts of protein in the diet, an idea that has proved to be
wrong. Only small quantities of protein are required to fulfill
either normal needs or those of the athlete, and American diets
are normally rich in protein. Furthermore, since protein cannot be stored for later use in building cells, there is no point in
deliberately consuming large quantities.

Though excessive amounts of protein are unnecessary and
can even be harmful, adequate protein is a vital nutritional
requirement. People in many parts of the world suffer permanent damage or die because of inadequate supplies of high-
quality protein. A living person produces over a million new
cells every second along with thousands of enzymes—complex
chemical regulators—that are needed to govern the chemical
reactions in each cell. A constant supply of protein is needed to
make both new cells and enzymes.

There are some important characteristics of protein that
need to be understood if you are on an unusual diet, particularly a vegetarian one. In order to be used for building tissue,

protein must be made up of a number of amino acids in just the right proportions to one another. When there are excesses of particular amino acids, they are either used as fuel or excreted as waste. Thus, if a food contains all the essential amino acids except one, none of the protein can be used for building tissue unless the missing amino acid is supplied by another food eaten at the same meal.

The reason that vegetarians have to be especially concerned with the proportions of amino acids—protein "quality"—is that most vegetable proteins, when eaten alone, are not well balanced for building human tissues. Animal proteins, dairy products, and eggs are fairly close to the mixture we need, so they are frequently said to contain "high quality" protein. But a proper combination of vegetable proteins can result in protein with just as high a quality. Traditional diets of people who live largely without meat include just such mixtures—corn and beans, for example. Those interested in vegetarian diets are referred to the list of additional reading for information on the proper combining of proteins.

VITAMINS AND MINERALS

In addition to fuel and protein for building new cells, the body needs small quantities of a number of other substances to survive and function properly. Some of these are simple minerals, like iron, potassium, and zinc. Others are vitamins: complex organic compounds that are required but that cannot be synthesized by the body. An inadequate supply of one of the vitamins or minerals will either produce immediate difficulties or eventually result in the more subtle symptoms of a deficiency disease. A deficiency in sodium and potassium can cause muscle cramping, for example. Insufficient iron over a period of time will result in anemia—a decline in the body's red blood cells. A deficiency of vitamin C among sailors who went for months without fresh foods used to cause scurvy, characterized by muscular weakness, rotting teeth, bleeding under the skin, and so forth. Over the years nutritionists have identified many vitamins and essential minerals, associated them with the deficiency diseases they prevent, and mapped out some of their functions.

The minimum daily requirement (MDR) of a vitamin is the amount that has been determined sufficient to prevent deficiency diseases from occurring. One can speculate, however, that more of a particular vitamin might be required for blooming good health than the minimum amount necessary to avoid deficiency diseases. This is officially recognized in the RDA, the recommended daily allowance as defined by the U.S. Food and Drug Administration, which is the amount that nutritionists feel it might be a good idea to consume each day.

There is probably no more controversial area of diet than that of vitamins. Do supplemental vitamins do the average person any good? Do they make the runner any healthier or help the body adapt to the stresses of training? Are vitamins from "natural" sources any better than those from "artificial" ones? Most professional nutritionists maintain that a normal balanced diet provides an ample supply of all the vitamins and trace minerals needed for good health or hard training. (The possible exception of iron for women is discussed separately below.) These experts maintain that taking massive doses of water-soluble vitamins like vitamin C has little effect other than to give the runner very expensive urine. They warn against fat-soluble vitamins such as vitamin A because these can accumulate in the body and because excessive amounts may be poisonous.

Advocates of selected usage of vitamins argue that the standard recommended doses are adequate to prevent deficiency diseases but that there is evidence that some vitamins in larger quantities are helpful in recuperation from the training stress of hard running. They also point out that few people in the modern world live in a natural environment and contend that selected vitamins help the body to deal with the toxins and artificial stress that are part of our world.

There is no simple way to settle any of these arguments definitively, particularly since the stresses referred to and the vitamins advocated vary a good deal. Anecdotal evidence on both sides is plentiful, but many of the controlled situations that are necessary for good scientific studies are difficult to apply to runners in the real world.

As an example of the difficulties, let's look for a moment at a simple mineral substance, salt. Common table salt is a relatively pure form of the chemical sodium chloride. When you consume it, it dissolves, and the ions of sodium and chlorine can act separately in the body, the more important of the two being sodium. Sodium is essential to the functioning of the body. It is one of the electrolytes* that serve all sorts of necessary purposes. Since salt is excreted in perspiration and in urine, some intake is necessary for the body to continue to function properly. Furthermore, salt is generally harmless even if taken in excess, since the extra amounts are disposed of in the urine and in sweating. For a runner in hot weather who secretes a lot of salt in sweating, it might seem wise to increase salt intake, and in fact salt tablets are still commonly taken by many athletes to prevent cramps during hot-weather exercise.

It turns out, however, that excess salt intake may be rather unhealthy; most natural-food advocates think so. It is definitely dangerous for people with certain diseases. Runners have also found that the body gets used to throwing off a great deal of salt when they sweat a lot, and this is what causes the body to lose too much salt in hot-weather running. Along with sodium, the body throws off potassium, another important electrolyte, which is not replaced by salt tablets. A properly acclimatized runner doesn't need extra salt, because the sweat is more dilute and little salt is lost. Many runners have even found that they acclimatize better and faster if they stay on a diet free of added salt all the time, relying on the small but adequate amounts found in many foods.

Similar problems exist with those vitamins for which there is

---

*Electrolytes are substances that will dissolve in water, splitting into a pair of oppositely charged particles that can carry current. Salt, for example, separates into a positively charged sodium ion and a negatively charged chlorine ion in solution. Electrolytes play many important roles in body chemistry.

some evidence in favor of large supplements. The best case is for vitamin C. There are some good reasons to believe that very large doses may help cure colds or alleviate symptoms; but the evidence is contradictory, and the medical establishment has been slow to do the necessary research. Many experts believe that runners should regularly take large doses of vitamin C to promote recovery from long training runs and to help prevent overuse injuries to the joints and tendons. Dr. Thomas Bassler of the American Medical Joggers Association recommends about a gram (twenty-two times the RDA) for every six miles of training. To get this from orange juice, a runner doing twelve miles a day would need to drink about a gallon, so most believers in this theory take vitamin C tablets.

The contrary argument that can be made against supplements is that people are adapted by evolution to heavy exercise and that they are not likely to have evolved with a need for quantities of vitamins that could not normally have been obtained from a natural diet. There have also been some reports of mild cases of scurvy occurring in people on a normal diet who had been taking vitamin C supplements for years and who then stopped taking them. One could make an analogy with salt and assume that their bodies were used to excreting the vitamin as waste, so that it was no longer used efficiently.

With this summary of the cases for and against vitamin supplements, I will leave the problem to the reader and summarize what is known about other vitamins for runners in training. As with vitamin C, a lot of research needs to be done. One thing that all responsible authorities agree on is that you should eat a balanced diet with lots of fresh fruits and vegetables. If you exist on junk food, you *do* need vitamin supplements, but they will not fully compensate for the deleterious effects of too many highly processed foods, sugar, and fat.

VITAMIN NEEDS

Vitamins can be subdivided as either water-soluble or fat-soluble. In general, supplementing your diet with water-soluble vitamins is less risky, because excess amounts are simply excreted in the urine. Fat-soluble vitamins should be treated more circumspectly because they can accumulate in the body. The primary water-soluble vitamins are vitamin C and the B complex of vitamins. Vitamin C has been discussed, and it probably has the best case for supplemental use by runners. Most of the B vitamins are widely available in foods and also synthesized by bacteria in the body, so deficiencies are extremely unlikely. The two B vitamins that deserve some special consideration are vitamins B_1 and B_{12}.

The body needs vitamin B_1 to utilize sugar, so deficiencies are possible if you eat a lot of highly processed foods and gobble large quantities of sweets, which is a temptation for runners in the evening after a hard workout. As long as you eat a reasonably balanced diet and don't overdo too often on sugar, you shouldn't have to worry about getting enough vitamin B_1. B_{12} is a vitamin that is plentiful in a normal diet but difficult to obtain on a strict vegetarian regimen—one that excludes dairy products, eggs, and fish as well as meat. Strict vegetarians need to pay particular attention to this vitamin. Since dairy products are a good source of B_{12} and a deficiency takes a long time to develop, vegetarians who use dairy products should not have any difficulty.

Fat-soluble vitamins include A, D, E, and K. A is an important vitamin that is widely available in fresh foods, both animal and vegetable. It is stored in the human liver, so deficiencies are unlikely to develop in any sensible diet. Vitamin A is definitely toxic in excessive quantities, so supplements containing more than the RDA should be avoided. D is classified by some nutritionists as a vitamin and by some as a hormone, because it is synthesized by humans who get reasonable exposure to sunlight, but not by people who don't get much sun. Runners are unlikely to develop a deficiency because they usually spend a good deal of time outdoors and because vitamin D is commonly added to a number of foods. Excessive quantities are toxic. Vitamin K is made by the bacteria that normally live in the intestines, so there is no likelihood of deficiency in normal circumstances. Vitamin E is currently a popular vitamin. It has been identified and isolated, and methods of manufacture have been developed, but no one has ever been able to produce a deficiency in humans even under clinical conditions, much less find one that exists naturally. (Deficiencies have been produced in animals.) This may be because we don't need vitamin E, or it may be because vitamin E is found in so many foods. No toxicity has been demonstrated, either, so there is probably no harm in supplements—though since E is a fat-soluble vitamin, at least a modicum of caution would seem advisable in avoiding large doses.

One point about additional vitamin requirements of runners during hard training is worth making. If you eat a balanced diet with plenty of fresh foods—especially fruits, vegetables, whole grains, and legumes—you will naturally get more vitamins when you increase your caloric intake, so that additional vitamin requirements take care of themselves. If you make up the energy deficit with sugar binges, however, you may develop some vitamin deficiencies. Use your common sense.

MINERAL REQUIREMENTS

Most minerals are supplied in ample quantities by a normal diet and require little thought on the part of the runner. As mentioned above, there can be large losses of salt and other electrolytes during heavy sweating, particularly in runners who have not acclimatized to hot-weather running. Electrolyte replacement drinks that contain the proper mixture to restore losses from sweating are useful during and after long runs in hot weather. Potassium replacement is particularly important if you use salt on your food. Orange juice is a good source, as are bananas. Commercially prepared electrolyte-replacement drinks are designed specifically to replace minerals lost in sweat.

Some authorities feel that magnesium losses during running are high enough to require special attention. Many foods contain some magnesium, but usually not in very large amounts.

Some runners take magnesium supplements. Good natural sources are brains, liver, seafood, egg yolks, nuts, and soybeans. Experiments in replacing magnesium in drinks while running have not been very successful, since the mineral is hard to assimilate quickly and can act as a laxative.

The mineral that deserves the most attention, particularly from women runners, is iron. There is some evidence that athletes generally have a greater-than-average need for iron, and the average American diet is not particularly rich in iron. Women who have not reached menopause have nearly twice the iron requirements of mature men even though they generally eat less, so women naturally suffer from iron deficiencies more often. Many authorities believe that a high percentage of women in the United States have mild anemia as a result of inadequate iron intake. Runners may be worse off still, and they will certainly be affected by the reduced oxygen-carrying capacity of anemic blood. Iron deficiencies for women and for adolescent runners of both sexes are therefore probably the only likely chronic dietary shortages among American runners who eat fairly sensibly.

There are a number of ways to make sure you get enough iron—iron supplements are an obvious possibility. Good natural sources are dried beans, lentils, liver, spleen, potato flour, rice bran, whole sesame seeds, blackstrap molasses, sorghum syrup, soybeans and soy flour, sunflower seeds, wheat bran, and wheat germ. Spinach, nuts, and regular cuts of meat supply less impressive amounts. One way to increase slightly the usable iron in your diet—believe it or not!—is to do a lot of your cooking in cast-iron cookware.

"NATURAL" AND VEGETARIAN DIETS

There is no doubt that the heavy processing of foods results in a loss of nutrients, so the less modification the food receives and the fresher it is when eaten, the more wholesome it is likely to be. The practice of replacing nutrients that have been removed with synthesized substitutes is a great improvement on not replacing them at all, but valuable food value is still quite likely to be lost. Highly refined, lily-white foods are likely to have surrendered all their food values except the calories. Nutritionists have recently recognized the importance of "fiber" in the diet, for example. Fiber is a general term for all that roughage and indigestible cellulose that is so plentiful in a diet that consists mainly of vegetable products. The food industry's answer has been to sell "high fiber" bread to which large amounts of wood pulp have been added instead of bread made with whole grains. This is the sort of insanity that advocates of natural food can point to in defense of strict adherence to a diet that avoids as much as possible the products of industrial food production.

On the other hand, many advocates of natural foods have made enough absurd claims to give ammunition to those claiming no advantages at all for natural diets. The truth lies somewhere in between. Since the ideal of a natural diet is to escape the numerous organically active chemicals and poisons that surround us in modern life, a pure test will remain impossible; residues of insecticides and hundreds of other compounds—some dangerous, some perhaps innocuous—seep into the remotest corners of the earth and the farthest reaches of the food chain. The real choice for the individual is the degree to which he or she wants to work to avoid such additives and contaminants.

There seems to be little doubt that a diet concentrating on fruits, vegetables, whole grains, nuts, legumes, and dairy products—perhaps supplemented with some fish, poultry, or lean meat—would be healthier than the average American diet. Other questions remain open: whether honey is healthier than sugar, or whether vegetables grown without artificial fertilizers are better for you than those grown organically, for example.

A well-planned strict vegetarian diet is also healthier than the average American diet, though it is again open to question whether it is any healthier than a similar diet with some modest amounts of meat included. The American medical establishment has shown little interest in studying such questions, and definitive answers are always hard to come by in such areas. But there are a number of advantages to a vegetarian diet that have been experienced by those who have tried it. These are worth our attention, even if they do not constitute valid scientific studies.

One undeniable advantage to a vegetarian diet is the ease with which a vegetarian can attain a healthy weight. Vegetarians generally have no problem losing excess fat while eating as much as they want. This is partly due to the fact that many of the foods eaten are naturally low in fat and calories. A number of vegetarian converts who have kept calorie counts have also noted that they lost weight even while eating the same number of calories as before. There are several possible explanations for these reports, and the experience may or may not prove to be a general one. Since a person on a vegetarian diet also commonly avoids such products as sugar, it is difficult to isolate the influence of a single factor.

If you decide to try a vegetarian diet, remember that to be healthy it needs to be varied, just as a conventional diet does. Paying attention to complementary proteins, discussed earlier, is important, particularly for those who are avoiding all animal products. Such persons also need to be sure they have some source of vitamin B_{12}. Several books listed in the bibliography are useful for those experimenting with vegetarian diets. As with most similar problems, though, the main difficulty involved is in changing the habits of a lifetime.

FUEL FOR RUNNING

The energy for running comes from energy that is stored in the chemical bonds of the food that we eat. Since you are not likely to be gobbling large quantities of food during a long run, it is clear that the fuel used must be stored in your body. The body can store reserve fuel in several places. Fats are stored in fatty excess tissue, mostly under the skin, as a long-term energy supply that can be mobilized in times of food shortage. Fatty acids can also be held in the bloodstream and in other places where they are readily mobilized to provide fuel for endurance effort. Efficient storage and mobilization of fats is apparently a primary factor in the capacity of the body to engage in extended heavy work, an ability that is not well developed in most modern Americans, even in many runners. Since the ability of the body to store carbohydrates is much more limited, fat metabolism must be relied on in long events like ultramarathons to provide the runner with a continuing source of energy. Fats are a much more concentrated fuel and can be stored in much greater quantities, so they are ideal for this purpose. But since fats require more oxygen to release their energy, the runner cannot move as fast while using fats as fuel as when using carbohydrates. Teaching the body to use fats effficiently has major advantages for the runner, however, both to make extended efforts possible and to conserve the limited storage bank of carbohydrates. Teaching the body to function efficiently on fat metabolism is one of the goals of extended distance training. Experience with fasting also seems to help in this respect.

The carbohydrates that we eat for fuel come in many complex forms, which the body breaks down into simple sugars for use as fuel. The muscles are fueled by molecules of glucose, which can be metabolized either in the efficient aerobic process if enough oxygen is available or in the inefficient anaerobic process if not enough oxygen can be supplied. A constant supply of glucose is maintained in the blood (blood sugar) for use where it is needed, but particularly to supply the brain and the nervous system with a constant source of fuel. The brain cannot use fat for fuel, and this is why a drop in blood sugar affects your mental processes so drastically. (The heart, on the other hand, is a model endurance muscle, and it is fueled by fats.) The blood-sugar level is maintained from the supply stored in the liver, as well as from new input from the digestive system.

The working muscles maintain their own separate banks of stored glucose in the form of long chains of linked glucose molecules called glycogen. As you run at your maximum aerobic pace, you are using up the stores of muscle glycogen that have been built up and kept ready for the purpose. Day-to-day training stimulates the working muscles to store as much glycogen as possible, one of the important training effects of regular running. Glycogen cannot be transferred from one muscle to another, so the particular muscles that receive regular endurance training are the ones that will build up glycogen-storage capacity. "The wall" experienced by runners in extended runs is simply the exhaustion of the glycogen stored in the working muscles, so that they have to switch to complete dependence on the slower process of fat metabolism.

Clearly, if you want to run fast for long distances, anything that can be done to increase the storage of glycogen in the working muscles or to conserve it during the run is to your advantage. The whole purpose of carbohydrate-loading diets, discussed in the next chapter, is to bring muscle glycogen to a maximum before an important distance race. Regular training teaches the muscles to use the limited supply more efficiently, to store more glycogen and to replenish supplies faster, and to eke out the glycogen available by using fats whenever possible.

This discussion presents only a simplified model of the way the body uses fuel for running. But understanding these simple factors and some of the details presented in the next chapter are helpful to the runner in understanding what is going on in training. Glycogen supplies take some time to replenish, for example, though the body can learn to rebuild supplies more rapidly. This is one of the main reasons why the runner takes some time to bounce back after a long, hard training run. There are other processes involved, too, but you can feel it when you run out of stored glycogen, and if you go out the next day and push hard, it will be apparent that the fuel supply in your muscles has not been completely replaced. Learning to feel the onset of these events can be useful both in gauging your training and in experimenting with techniques like carbohydrate loading. The feeling of having low blood sugar is also easily recognizable once you have experienced it a few times and understand what is going on in the body.

One of the secondary benefits of long-term running is an increased awareness of the many interrelated functions of the body. Eating and drinking no longer seem to be aspects of life that are separated from your running and other daily activities, because you learn to feel the effects of one upon the other. This is why so many long-term runners eventually become interested enough in a better diet to change the eating habits they have learned since childhood, and decide to switch to more natural foods and perhaps to a vegetarian diet. When you are sufficiently in tune with the physical workings of your body, you can *feel* what is good for you and what is not, in many respects. The long-time runner who has converted to a more natural diet may recognize that while scientific evidence cannot yet prove that such a diet is superior, the evidence of the body's responses is quite adequate for an individual verdict. Most people who have been running for a long time change at least some of their eating patterns for these same reasons. We have our own built-in laboratories if we pay attention to the evidence.

CHAPTER XII

CARBOHYDRATE LOADING

THE PRACTICE OF increasing muscle stores of glycogen prior to a big race with a special sequence of exercise and dieting changes has become fairly widespread, and the physiological principles involved are important even for runners who do not choose to "load" or "pack." This chapter will consider the theory behind the regimen, some of the problems associated with it, and a few variations that may prove useful.

Remember that there are several sources of fuel that the runner can use during a long run or a race, and that fuel depletion is often one of the limiting factors in performance. The ideal fuels for fast running are the sugars stored in the body or supplied during running, because less oxygen is required to produce energy from them than from the free fatty acids in the blood. Fat metabolism is still important, both for longer runs and to reduce the rate of depletion of sugar supplies during runs ranging from ten miles to the marathon; the increasing of the body's ability to utilize fat for fuel is discussed more extensively in the next chapter. Basically, however, the capacity to

168

metabolize fat for fuel during endurance exercise seems to be stimulated by extensive training at long distances, during which the supply of stored sugars is depleted.

There are three possible sources for sugar to provide energy during a run. Much of it is obtained from glycogen stores within the working muscle. (Remember that glycogen is essentially a chain of glucose molecules.) Muscle glycogen is an important source of fuel for runners of all distances and accounts for most of the energy used by the runner during the first half-hour of exercise. Thus, in events of five miles or less, stored muscle glycogen is the only really significant source of energy. As a race continues, the muscles begin to derive energy from blood glucose as well. The concentration of glucose in the bloodstream—blood sugar—is maintained by the liver, either from its own stores of glycogen or from carbohydrate sources sent to the liver from the digestive tract during exercise, such as glucose or sucrose from sweet drinks.

Of these three possible sources—feedings during exercise, glycogen stored in the muscles, and glycogen stored in the liver—two are limited to what has been accumulated prior to the race, and the third is limited by the capacity of the body to absorb food during heavy exercise. There is a good deal of controversy both among athletes and among scientists over how much glucose can be absorbed during a race and how much sugar, if any, should be added to drinks. This question is discussed in the next section. But regardless of whether you take sugar during a race, even if you manage to absorb it instead of merely retaining it in your stomach, only a very tiny percentage of the energy you use in a race can be supplied in this way. During short races there is no time to absorb anything from the gut, and during a long race vastly greater quantities of energy are required than can be taken up. Therefore you have to rely on a combination of stored fats and stored glycogen supplies for nearly all the energy used in the race. (Ingested glucose or other sugars can be important in other ways, such as restoring blood sugar levels required by the brain, which may drop during endurance events; but nearly all the fuel used by the muscles comes from stored sources.) The supplies of fat stored by the body are very large (sometimes too large), and their depletion is not a problem. The quantities of glycogen that can be stored are quite limited, however, and so are the ways in which they can be utilized. Glycogen stored in the muscle tissue can be used only by the muscles in which it is actually deposited. Glycogen stored in your arms cannot be used by your legs during a marathon. Thus, the working muscles of the legs can obtain glucose only from their own glycogen supplies or from the blood sugar released from the liver.

During short runs, the actual supply of fuel is not a limiting factor in performance. In a five-mile race, no trained athlete will run out of fuel for the muscles. Stored muscle glycogen will easily suffice to supply the needed energy. During endurance events, however, the limited quantities of glycogen that can be stored in the muscles are frequently depleted. This is when you hit the wall and slow down. If you also deplete your liver glycogen supplies enough so that blood-sugar level drops, you will begin to feel lightheaded, dizzy, and uncoordinated as your nervous system becomes inadequately supplied with fuel.

Since sugars can be utilized with less oxygen than fats can and since they are also critical to the functioning of the nervous system, it stands to reason that the endurance athlete will be better off if more glycogen is stored in the working muscles and the liver. These supplies vary, depending on both long- and short-term dietary and exercise practices. If you run a lot, your body will adapt and will not run out of fuel so soon. Runners who regularly do extended training runs that deplete their supplies of glycogen adapt better to endurance situations and run down later in long races. What the athlete does in the days just before a race also has important effects, however. The idea of the carbohydrate-loading diets and their various modifications is to stimulate the working muscles and the liver to store the maximum amount of glycogen, so that the possibility of running out of sugar and hitting the wall is reduced or postponed until later in the race. Even those who do not pack need to pay some attention to their training and diet during the days before a long race like a marathon to insure that they have adequate supplies of glycogen.

SUPERCOMPENSATION

Two Swedish scientists discovered in the 1960's that if a working muscle was exercised heavily, depleting its reserves of glycogen, and then kept depleted for several days, it would respond by supercompensating if given adequate carbohydrate supplies afterward. That is, it would respond by storing not only the usual quantities of glycogen but an extra amount as well. This was the beginning of the various carbohydrate loading, carbohydrate packing, or supercompensation regimens. The Swedish research and that of other scientists since has shown that moderately well-trained athletes do achieve better times in long-distance races after following a carbohydrate-loading diet. Before discussing its advantages, disadvantages, and possible modifications, we should review the standard packing sequence.

The first step in the normal loading routine is to take a very long run six or seven days prior to the race for which you are packing. This serves to deplete the glycogen supplies of the working muscles. The length of the depletion run depends on your speed and on your own normal training, but it has to be long enough to thoroughly exhaust muscle glycogen. Experienced runners can usually tell when this has occurred. It is generally better at this stage in training to take a long, moderately paced run. Too fast a pace risks injury or exhaustion close to an important long race. (If the race is significantly less than twenty miles, a properly trained runner will not run out of muscle glycogen anyway, and packing is pointless.)

During the next three days, the runner trains only moderately (and miserably) and stays on a diet that is very low in digestible carbohydrates. The emphasis is on foods that contain primarily protein, fat, and cellulose. (The cellulose in vegetables like celery is carbohydrate, but it passes through the digestive tract without yielding up much energy, providing necessary roughage only.) The low-carbohydrate diet combined with moderate training keeps the muscle glycogen depleted through the three days following the depletion run.

Finally, during the last three days before the long race the runner switches to a diet that is rich in carbohydrates. It is important that this should not be a high-calorie diet. Loading does not mean loading up on food. It is simply a normal quantity of food that consists mainly of items like grains, pasta, fruit, bread, cereals, and vegetables that are high in carbohydrates and relatively low in fat and protein. The muscles that have been kept very low in glycogen for several days after the depletion run react by storing far more glycogen than they normally would. During this period the runner trains very lightly or not at all, so that the glycogen being stored is not depleted. The packer will gain a couple of pounds above normal weight because of the large amounts of water stored with the glycogen; a somewhat tight or bloated feeling in the muscles is common. This liquid becomes available to the body during the race, though it has to be carried along for the first few miles.*

SOME OBJECTIONS

There are a number of problems with packing regimens. They disrupt and dictate your training during the crucial week prior to a big race, and such interference can be detrimental both physiologically and psychologically. The low-carbohydrate phase of the diet is unnatural and unpleasant, flying in the face of common sense and the natural desires of your body. You want and need carbohydrates. There are some demonstrable dangers to this extreme diet, though these are minimal to the well-trained athlete who is otherwise healthy and who keeps up an adequate intake of liquids through the whole routine. (The full loading regimen should never be used by people who are inadequately trained for the race they are planning or by those

---

*Evidence suggests that this regimen also stimulates supercompensation in the liver, but this has not been conclusively demonstrated.

with liver or kidney ailments.) Running during the low-carbohydrate phase is miserable because of glycogen depletion.

Loading regimens are hard to time correctly. People reach peak supercompensation at different rates. Regular experience of depletion, as in fasting and long runs, seems to teach the body to supercompensate more quickly. More experienced runners, especially those who load or fast regularly, are likely to find that they reach their peak glycogen storage in only a couple of days. After the peak, the muscles unload the extra glycogen, a phase signaled by loose bowels, a lot of urination, and the loss of the extra weight and the tight-legged feeling that accompanies supercompensation. Reaching supercompensation twenty-four hours too early means that the athlete goes through all the unpleasantness and disruption of the regimen without having any of its benefits at race time.

The most telling objection to carbohydrate loading is that it puts added and unfamiliar stress on the body just when you are trying to fine-tune and gather up your reserves. In addition, it can be argued that at least in races of marathon length or less, the properly trained runner doesn't generally hit the wall—that good training will extend one's crash point out past 26 miles, 385 yards. The counterargument is that the assurance of maximum glycogen reserves prevents the combination of fast pace, environmental factors, and low glycogen from slowing the runner badly at an unexpected point.*

---

*Dr. Joan Ullyot has argued that women do not hit the wall as men do during long races. She feels that this is because women have a better capacity to metabolize fats, and so they can better eke out their glycogen reserves. This point has been argued strongly on both sides. But as women run marathon distances faster, it is beginning to appear that quite a few of them are hitting the wall, too. I would guess that the best-trained women have not run all-out in the past and so were less likely to hit the wall. Other women marathoners, who were less well trained, were also more sensible than their male counterparts at the same conditioning level and less likely than the men to go out too fast. A number of women runners at the 1979 New York Marathon, where Grete Waitz set a new world record of 2:27:33, showed the classic symptoms of hitting the wall, and all the top women were running at paces faster than the women's world record of just a few years ago.

RULES FOR LOADING

If you decide to try carbohydrate loading for a major race, there are a few fairly simple rules that are important to using the system effectively. I would suggest that you try one of the modified plans suggested below first to gain some familiarity with loading while avoiding some of the more disruptive aspects. Older runners are particularly well advised to try one of the milder regimens, since they are more likely to have trouble with the full sequence. It is best to try it out on a training run or low-key race a couple of months before an important race.

Keep the initial depletion run to a comfortable pace. Full depletion is important in order to achieve supercompensation, but it is not as crucial as avoiding injury or major fatigue a week before a big race. Use a low-carbohydrate diet that is also low in calories. Don't eat large quantities of fatty foods. Yogurt, chicken, fish, cheese, eggs, celery, and leafy salad with vinegar-and-oil dressing are good foods to include. By keeping the quantities down you will avoid some of the bad effects of the diet, reduce your weight somewhat, and lessen the temptation to overeat when you switch to the high-carbohydrate phase. Some people overeat during the low-carbohydrate period, probably because they are craving carbohydrates that they aren't getting. Eat a few carbohydrates during this phase to help avoid the effects of low blood sugar—perhaps two or three medium-sized pieces of fruit or small glasses of juice a day. Drink plenty of water, at least three quarts a day, and run five miles a day or so to stay depleted.

You can judge your level of depletion well from the way you feel during these runs. If you are very slow and washed out, then your muscles are thoroughly depleted. A final redepletion run should be taken the day before you commence the high-carbohydrate diet. Traditionally this run is seven to ten miles long, but it only needs to be long enough for you to thoroughly redeplete. If you feel wrung out in the first mile or two, a run of five or six miles will be enough.

Be sure to drink lots of water and eat plenty of fruits and other sources of potassium during the carbohydrate-loading phase of the regimen. Added potassium is important during loading. It is the percentage of carbohydrates that determines the degree of supercompensation, not the quantity, so eat moderately. Light meals together with a number of small snacks give the best results. Watching your weight will give you a good idea of what is happening. You should gain several pounds during the supercompensation phase. Be sure to drink large quantities of juices and water, since inadequate hydration will reduce the desired effect of the diet and can have very dangerous side-effects. You should train very little during this phase, since running will reduce the supercompensation.

MODIFIED LOADING TECHNIQUES

There are a number of modifications of the standard loading sequence that have many of the same beneficial effects while eliminating some of the stressful elements of the original technique. The most disruptive part of the standard sequence is the depletion phase, during which the runner trains in spite of a low consumption of carbohydrates. This part of the loading regimen is both psychologically and physically disturbing. One modification is simply to eliminate the depletion phase altogether. Continue to run through the first part of the week before the race, and then reduce your training load to a very light one, switching to a diet consisting almost completely of carbohydrates. As with the full routine, you should not overeat and you should get plenty of liquids, including lots of fruit juice. This routine definitely results in a substantial increase in glycogen stores in the muscles by race day, though the increase will not be as pronounced as it is with the full depletion schedule.

This short schedule can also be used with a long depletion run just before the high-carbohydrate loading phase. If you are running a marathon on Sunday, for example, a long run is done on Wednesday morning to deplete the muscles' glycogen

reserves. Very few carbohydrates are eaten for the rest of the
day on Wednesday. (I recommend fasting, as in the longer
method described below.) A high-carbohydrate diet with plenty
of fluids is eaten on Thursday, Friday, and Saturday, with only
light training being done. This schedule will probably result in
glycogen levels at least twice as high as normal, though not
quite as high as with the full routine. One obvious problem is
that it requires a very long run only a few days before a major
race. If the run is not hard enough, full depletion won't result;
and if it is too hard, you run the risk of overwork with insufficient time for recovery.

I think that experienced runners who do regular extended
training workouts that use up their glycogen reserves probably
excrete large amounts of the enzymes responsible for glycogen
storage even without the full depletion regimen. For them, the
most important aspects of the loading system are the several
days of rest before a long, important race together with the
high-carbohydrate diet. The combination allows the muscles to
build up their glycogen stores instead of using them up in
training. This modified loading procedure is essentially the
routine followed by many top marathoners and ultramarathoners before big races.

There are two other possible techniques which include a long
depletion phase but avoid some of the extremes and unpleasantness of the original sequence. One is simply to reduce your
food intake, emphasizing low-carbohydrate foods at the same
time, but not attempting to restrict carbohydrates radically. By
running a long depletion workout at the beginning of the week
and a moderate distance each of the next three days, the muscles can be kept fairly well depleted without nearly so much discomfort as in the normal depletion phase of the loading
schedule. The second phase, with a carbohydrate-rich diet and
very light workouts, is identical in all the schedules.

Still another method—the one I consider the most comfortable to follow if you want to try the full depletion stage—is to
fast for the three days following the initial depletion run. Moderate workouts are done during this period, and the switch-
over to a high-carbohydrate diet and very light training is then

made. I find fasting a good deal more comfortable than the artificial high-fat, high protein diets, and I suspect it is healthier as well. Hunger is largely suppressed by the normal fasting mechanisms described in the next chapter, and I find moderate running to be much more pleasant on a fast than during a low carbohydrate diet. Why this is so, I cannot be sure, but it may be that production of the enzymes used by the body for promoting fat metabolism is stimulated when you are fasting more than when you are on the low-carbohydrate diet. I prefer a juice fast, as described in the next chapter, rather than a strict water fast, but the juices should probably be diluted for this purpose. I think that if you use two parts water to one part juice, you can drink as much as you like and still gain all the benefits of the depletion stage. Drinking at least some juice reduces the possibility of dangerously low blood sugar during training runs and helps to replace minerals lost in sweating.

THE REST PHASE

One of the most difficult questions about carbohydrate-loading diets is what to do about training during the week. There is no question that you should reduce training during the last three days before a long major race. (Remember that loading is worthless for shorter races, anyway.) The body needs rest as well as time to build up glycogen storage. Most of the researchers on supercompensation recommend complete rest, however, and it is open to question whether this is really a good idea. It may be that detraining effects from lack of exercise more than offset the benefits of the extra glycogen supplies that result. Personally, I feel that some light running the day before a race is a good idea even if glycogen storage is slightly reduced. I prefer a rest day two or three days before the race and easy five-mile runs on the other two days.

EXPERIMENTING

It is difficult to use any of these schedules without some experimentation, and one of the problems with them is that they are disruptive enough so that it isn't a good idea to use them very often. The body also modifies its responses if loading is practiced frequently. People react so differently, however, depending on their training practices, conditioning, and individual metabolism, that it is impossible to find out how loading will affect you without trying various methods out. I would suggest gaining some experience with the short methods prior to a couple of races in the fifteen-to-twenty-mile range. These methods may not result in quite as much supercompensation as the long ones, but they will build quite adequate supplies for these shorter races. If you find these experiences helpful, you might want to try one of the longer methods.

If you try the shorter techniques, you should observe carefully how rapidly you build up your glycogen supplies. Many runners who do extensive distance, especially if they fast occasionally, will find that they reach full supercompensation in two days rather than three. The schedules have to be modified accordingly. If you lose the weight you have gained and get loose bowels on the third day of the high-carbohydrate diet, you should not start this phase until two days before the big race.

CHAPTER XIII

FASTING

FASTING PROVIDES AN interesting contrast to carbohydrate loading. Though a few athletes used techniques similar to carbohydrate loading in the past, the procedure was basically the creation of physiological researchers. Fasting, however, has a long tradition of use among mystics, athletes, and health fanatics, but until recently it has been ignored or pooh-poohed by most physicians and nutritionists. Another contrast between carbohydrate loading and fasting is in their effects on the body. Carbohydrate-loading procedures may have had some good nutritional side effects for runners by pointing up the need for emphasis on carbohydrates in the diet as a whole. This has provided a useful antidote to the protein mythology that most of us were raised on. We have learned that protein needs are really quite low, for athletes and everyone else. Basically, however, carbohydrate loading is a form of self-abuse pointed toward racing performance. Whether it is effective or not, the depletion phase cannot possibly be good for you. Fasting, on the other hand, may have some very beneficial effects.

Unfortunately, very little is known about the precise effects of fasting on an athlete in training, particularly the effects of regular fasting. Research on fasting is scanty at best, and much of the literature is on the physiology of fasting for obese, unhealthy, inactive people. As with everything else, people believe what they want to believe. Most nutritionists and physicians dismiss the claims of fasting advocates as dangerous nonsense. The most knowledgeable experts on fasting have tended to mix their scientific data with enthusiastic claims rather indiscriminately, so that it is impossible to isolate established facts from unsubstantiated assertions.

Most of the rest of this chapter therefore falls into the category of opinion. Until more work has been done, the only way you are likely to find out how fasting will affect you and your running is to try it.

WHAT HAPPENS DURING FASTING

Fasting is not starvation, except in individuals who are already so light that they have virtually no stored fat on their bodies. Experts on long fasts note that there is a distinct change in sensations when the point of starvation is reached. Hunger returns in the form of craving for food, described as a sensation in the mouth rather than the gnawing in the stomach that most people associate with hunger. I have never fasted long enough to have experienced this change personally, but I can testify to the usual experience of the complete disappearance of normal hunger and craving for food. Everyone who has tried fasting has found that hunger is not a problem after a fairly short initial period. I lose my hunger after a day; some report that this occurs after two or three days. It isn't really very hard to maintain a fast. Compared with all the agonies that many people experience during normal low-calorie dieting, fasting is almost trivially easy, especially for runners. Running helps to suppress the appetite during the initial period of the fast.

You do not have to stop running while fasting; quite the contrary. Instinct may tell us that fasting is hard, that physical activity during a fast should be very difficult, and so on, but it just isn't so! Every runner I have talked with who has tried fasting has found it easy and enjoyable to maintain a normal training schedule while fasting. Most agree that hard workouts at the edge of ragged fatigue should be avoided, but there is no need to reduce the pace of your normal distance work during a fast.

There are two basic schools of fasting. The traditional, true fast is a water fast. You eat nothing and drink nothing except water. Most runners who practice and advocate fasting use juice fasting instead, and the statements made in the rest of this chapter refer to juice fasting. The quantities of juice consumed vary, but the basic reason for drinking at least some juice is to provide a few carbohydrates in a readily assimilated liquid form. This avoids the danger of radical drops in the level of blood sugar, which cause dizziness, blackouts, and possible damage to the brain and nervous system. The body increases its reliance on stored fat and its use of protein from sources within the body during a fast, but it cannot manufacture the sugars needed by the nervous system. Juices have the additional advantage of replacing minerals and vitamins lost through perspiration during training runs. I would recommend avoiding pure water fasts. If you do try one, gain some experience with juice fasts first.

Fasting is the quickest way to lose weight. It is particularly effective for runners, because the combination of fasting and training will burn off extra fat very quickly. The experience of fasting runners has been that fasting for reasonable periods— at least up to a week—does not result in any deterioration in performance due to muscle wasting. On the contrary, they report improved performance. There is no doubt that people who have significant fat on their bodies obtain most of their energy during a fast from consumption of that stored fat. Researchers do report, however, that the body also consumes some protein from the muscles. Major consumption of working tissues by the body does not occur until the stored fat has been used up—a long time for most of us. Advocates of fasting maintain that exercising individuals conserve the working tissues and do not experience muscle wasting even to the extent that inactive people do. I think that this assertion is probably true, but there is not enough research to prove it.

Runners fast for other reasons than to lose weight, however. A number of runners competing at distances ranging from sprints to ultramarathons have experimented with fasting prior to important races and have often been very pleased with the results. Some have fasted for periods of as long as a week preceding their races. Park Barner, America's greatest modern ultramarathoner, uses fasting frequently prior to long races and shatters records right and left. How can this sort of experience be reconciled with the carbohydrate-loading and depletion theories? Barner runs 50-milers at a pace faster than a 3-hour marathon pace. How does he do it? Perhaps he is simply so efficient that he can run at speeds like this using fat metabolism almost exclusively, and his fasting helps to shift the body over to efficient use of fats. He is known as a noncompetitive runner and may simply run far below the pace at which he needs to burn a lot of sugar. Barner is certainly as far removed from most of us in ability as Bill Rodgers and Frank Shorter are—he holds the U.S. 24-hour record at just under 153 miles, and he ran a 50-mile race the day after setting that record—but the fact is that the research has just not been done that will answer such questions. Could Bill Rodgers run a sub-2:10 marathon while fasting? No one really knows. The normal theories would deny the possibility, but there are a lot of other performances that people have accomplished while fasting that seem to violate the theories, too.

Fasting is essentially rather benign and has been used frequently as part of the treatment for various diseases. It does have dangers, however, and I would not recommend that anyone who is not already in good condition fast while running. By the same token, anyone who has medical problems of any kind should not fast without consulting a physician. For the healthy, well-conditioned runner, however, fasting for reasonable periods should not be considered an extreme activity. The one dietary characteristic common to those human populations that have exceptionally long lives seems to be that they eat very little. We need a lot less food than we think we do.

CLAIMS FOR FASTING

Advocates of fasting believe that it not only helps the runner to lose or maintain low weight but it also helps you to run better. They feel that it helps teach the body to metabolize fats more efficiently and to store them in more easily retrieved form. They argue that when you fast, your body consumes not only stored fat but old and superfluous tissue as well, using moribund cells as raw material to build new ones and ridding the body of waste. They maintain that by temporarily eliminating the effort of processing and digesting food, your energies can be turned to other purposes, giving the digestive system a rest and allowing diseased cells, waste, and pollutants to be purged from the body.

Whether or not any or all of these contentions are true, the subjective experiences of many runners seem to bear them out. All the runners with whom I have spoken who have tried fasting felt better during and after their fasts and plan to try longer fasts in the future. This is wholly unscientific evidence, of course. If we think that something is going to make us feel better, it often does so simply because of our positive anticipation. Scientific studies are difficult to conduct in areas like fasting, particularly on subjective questions like running performance and feelings of physical well-being. This tends to make researchers shy away from the interesting questions about fasting.

It follows that if you want to find out whether fasting will make you feel any better or improve your running, you will have to try it out and see for yourself. Scientific testing may one day bear out some of the subjective reports offered by fasters, and refute others, but in the meantime we have only the testimony of those who have tried fasting techniques as part of their training together with our own experiences.

SOME RECOMMENDATIONS

Fasting should be approached conservatively. It is a mistake for a runner to embark suddenly on a two-week fast with neither experience nor supervision. Increased metabolism of fats can build up dangerous waste products in the bloodstream and cause changes in the acidity of the body. If you decide to try fasting, start off with one-day fasts and work up to longer ones carefully, noting the effects on your running and on your general physical and emotional state. Run efficiently when you are training, and avoid bash days. Be cautious in experimenting with tempo running and races during long fasts.

Drink plenty of water whenever you are fasting. It is necessary both to maintain adequate hydration and to flush out wastes from the body. Drink as much diluted fruit juice as you want. Straight fruit juices can be hard on your stomach when you are fasting, but a variety of juices diluted somewhat with water will help to provide vitamins, minerals, and enough sugar to supply the nervous system. Light broth and herb tea are also fine to drink when you are fasting. Most authorities recommend that you avoid either coffee or regular tea when fasting, though I have occasionally drunk these in moderation when on a fast without any harmful effect.

Fasting for longer than a week or ten days should be taken much more seriously than short fasts. Muscle wasting and buildups of toxins are certainly more likely. I suggest that you avoid any long fasts unless you've had a good deal of experience. Consider obtaining supervision from someone who is knowledgeable about long fasts.

Fasting for moderate periods definitely seems beneficial for well-trained runners. Unlike other dietary manipulations, it has prompted reports from those who have tried it that are too uniformly enthusiastic to be discounted. It seems particularly beneficial for the specialist in very long distances. On the other hand, don't expect miracles from fasting. It won't substitute for training or make a slow runner fast. It is simply another element that has been a helpful training tool and an educational experience for many runners.

CHAPTER XIV

AVOIDING INJURY

THE MOST IMPORTANT rules for avoiding injuries have been emphasized throughout this book. The great majority of injuries are caused by training and racing errors, pushing the body beyond its limits for adaptation to stress, and ignoring the usual warning signs that precede most serious problems. Trying to race too soon after coming off one injury or after recovering from an illness is a frequent cause of more disastrous ailments. By heeding the symptoms of overstress listed in Chapter VI and by paying attention to chronic complaints before they become major, you will be able to head off most of the causes of runners' maladies before they start. Proper stretching and warming up before doing any hard speed work are also important. A basic set of stretches is illustrated later in this chapter.

There are a few other common sources of injuries among runners that deserve special attention, however, since understanding them now will save you a lot of trouble later on. Runners' injuries are mostly those of overuse. That is, they occur

185

when some particular link in the running apparatus is constantly stressed beyond its limits and finally gives way. If you bend a piece of copper wire once, it won't break, and even bending it back and forth several times won't usually cause it to come apart. Bend it again and again in the same place, though, and it will finally develop fatigue cracks and snap in two. Unlike the wire, the body can heal itself after each stress and even strengthen those areas that are beginning to weaken, but too much strain repeated too often will cause something to give. Such overuse injuries can result either from the sort of overtraining errors already mentioned or from other factors that cause excessive stress to be placed repeatedly on particular parts of the feet, joints, or legs. These factors can include badly designed or maintained shoes, poor running habits, insufficient flexibility, imbalanced strength between opposing muscles or between the muscles in the two legs, or abnormalities in the structure of the legs, feet, or spine.

In evaluating overuse injuries it is often difficult to separate the cause from other factors that may have contributed. Such injuries are often the result of a number of different stresses acting together, so there really is no single cause. Thus, a particular surge in training combined with feet that roll over excessively might cause a tendon or knee injury that could have been prevented either by a slower buildup or by orthotic foot supports. Once the injury occurs, however, both supports and a slower increase in stress may be required to permit the athlete to regain strength without getting hurt again. Overuse injuries are frustrating because they often take time and patience to heal and because so many factors may underlie them that they are hard to analyze. When possible, prevention is far better than cure.

MUSCULAR IMBALANCES

One cause of injuries that falls slightly outside the pattern of true overuse syndromes is a major difference in strength between complementary groups of muscles. Such imbalances can cause muscle pulls, particularly in doing speed work or racing. If the hamstrings are significantly stronger in one leg than in the other, for example, fast running is quite likely to cause a pulled muscle. Such problems often become chronic when runners return to training without a proper stretching and strengthening of the injured muscle during recovery, so that there is an even greater imbalance and the muscle is torn again. There is good research showing that runners with such muscle imbalances are far more likely to suffer pulls than those with equally strong legs.

Major imbalance between the muscles at the front and the back of the legs can also cause muscle pulls. The front group of muscles in the thigh—the quadriceps—should be about 50 percent stronger than those at the back—the hamstrings. If the quadriceps are significantly stronger than that, hamstring pulls will probably result, especially during speed work, when the hamstrings are forcibly extended during the kick. The quadriceps are somewhat less vulnerable because they are not stretched so much, but excessively strong hamstrings can make them more subject to muscle pulls. A muscle that is much weaker than its opposite also becomes less flexible, because the opposing muscle tires quickly and reduces movement. The running gait is distorted as a result, especially during long races.

Distance training tends to overdevelop all the muscles at the back of the legs at the expense of the muscles at the front. Sprinters tend to overdevelop the quadriceps, however, and this is one reason why they are more susceptible to hamstring pulls than distance runners are. Participants in other sports that develop the quadriceps heavily can experience hamstring pulls if they begin running. Friends of mine who do a lot of hard bicycle riding often have this problem when they return to running.

Unless you are doing regular weight training so that you know the relative strength of your leg muscles, it makes sense to check this factor occasionally, particularly before starting in on a major period of sharpening and speed training. The easiest method is to get access to a universal weight machine or to a weight bench that has an attachment for leg curls. Any gym with weight equipment, or a friend who does much weight training, will probably have such equipment. A weight boot may also be used. It is possible to improvise equipment at home if you can't find any available facilities.

You should be able to lift the same weight approximately the same number of times doing leg curls with both legs. (A leg curl requires you to lift a weight by bending your knee from a straight position to a fully flexed one against resistance.) Leg extension with a weight—the straightening of the knee from a bent position while you are either lying down or sitting—is the complementary quadriceps exercise. The quadriceps should be of equal strength and should be 1½ times as strong as the hamstrings. The hamstrings should also both be equally strong. If these tests show major imbalances, you should exercise the weak muscles regularly with weights or other devices three times a week until the muscles are equalized.

Muscle strength imbalances can also contribute to overuse injuries, and the exercises below are designed to prevent these. Some knee injuries can be cured or alleviated somewhat by strengthening weak quadriceps muscles. Weak muscles in the front of the lower leg are a frequent cause of shinsplints, and they often contribute to other problems like pain in the arch. Strengthening weak muscles in the feet and ankles can often reduce the incidence and severity of overuse injuries caused by abnormalities in the feet. Exercising the muscles in the front of the lower legs and in the ankles and feet therefore provides a first line of defense against many overuse injuries. (See exercise sequence in Chapter VIII.)

STRETCHING

Proper stretching is one of the most important preventive measures the runner can take against injuries. Distance running tends to shorten the muscles along the back of the body, particularly in the legs; and these are muscles that are already

One of the best methods to stretch the calves and Achilles tendons is to stand on an inclined board. As your muscles loosen up, lean forward and increase the tilt a little. Read a book for a while and really loosen these muscles.

Stretching the shins and the top of the foot. Hold this position for a while with each leg to get a good stretch before proceeding to the next position.

Starting with the shin stretch above, push the leg out and pull back until you feel the quadriceps stretch. Hold until they loosen and then stretch a little farther. With all stretches, you should feel a good pull in the muscle but *never* pain. As the muscle loosens, you can stretch farther. Never bounce or force a stretch.

Stretching the upper hamstrings. Grasp the knee and the heel and pull the leg up as a unit until you feel a good stretch in the upper hamstrings. Don't put too much leverage on the knee. This exercise stretches the back of the leg and the hip, not the knee.

The plough, with legs straight, stretches the back and the hamstrings. The weight of the body aids this stretch, so move very slowly to the limit of your comfort, concentrating on relaxing and breathing regularly. As with all these stretches, you may be able to stretch more or less than in the position shown. The photos are of an average tight runner who has not been stretching very long.

Stretching the lower hamstrings and the neck. Move your hand slowly down your leg until you feel a good stretch in the back of your leg above the knee. Keep both knees straight. Try to look up at your outstretched thumb. You may be able to slide your hand only partway down your leg, or you may be able to flatten your palm on the ground. Stretch your stiffer leg first, hold until the muscle relaxes, and stretch a little more.

Stretching the back. *Don't do this stretch if you have back trouble.* Push yourself up slowly on your arms and reach your face toward the sky.

Stretching out the groin muscles. Spread your legs as far as you can, comfortably, lock your knees, and bend toward the ground. Let comfort be your guide.

unusually tight in most adult Americans. I recommend stretching a couple of times a day, more often if you are having trouble with an injury or are unusually tight from heavy workouts. Most stretches can be done at any time during the day, and they make a good way to relax when you are tense. Once you form a habit of stretching regularly, you will find it is easy to work it into your daily pattern. Most runners who put off stretching simply haven't gotten into the routine. There are many good stretches for the important muscle groups of the body. The following illustrations show one set of possibilities.

SHOES

Good shoes that are well maintained provide another major insulator against injuries. Shoes have improved so much over the last few years that a much greater number of people are now able to run high mileages without injury or the use of specially constructed supports. It is important to find shoes that fit your feet well, provide proper support, and cushion your legs against the impact of running on hard surfaces. Different brands work better for different people, and the models change frequently, so only a few general principles for selection of shoes will be mentioned here.

A good fit is essential. No matter how well a shoe is designed or how many fine features it has, it has to fit your foot to do any good. Feet are shaped differently, and you will probably find that some brands fit you well, while others just aren't shaped correctly for your feet. Most brands come in only one width, so if your feet are wider or narrower than average, investigate the brands that offer varying widths, such as New Balance, Brooks, and Etonic. A shoe should fit snugly without constricting. Your feet will swell somewhat during a long, hot run. Your toes should not bang against the front of the toe counter when you push your foot forward in the shoe, particularly if you plan to run trails. Your foot shouldn't slide back and forth or from side to side in the shoe. Whether or not you wear socks when running, the shoe should feel smooth and comfortable inside without socks. Socks should not be so heavy as to affect fit significantly, except perhaps for shoes that will be used in very cold, sloppy conditions. (I use older shoes that have stretched a bit in these circumstances, with moderately heavy wool socks.) Normally, if you wear socks, light wool or bulked orlon works best.

The sole of the shoe should be flexible in the area of the ball of the foot. If you can't bend the toe up readily with a couple of fingers, reject the shoes. Stiff soles can help to precipitate several types of overuse injuries, placing unnatural stress on the muscles with each step. The heel should provide good cushioning. It should feel soft when you run in the shoe to try it out and should be fairly easy to indent with your thumbs. Department-store shoes often have inflexible soles with heels that are hard as a rock. The soft heel is necessary to compensate for the unnatural impact of running on hard surfaces.

Your foot should have good support. You can feel this if you put the shoes on and try to rock your feet around in them. Sloppy shoes allow your feet to move around a good deal. Support in the arch area is particularly important if your feet pronate excessively,* a condition usually referred to as flatfeet. Most people with flatfeet actually have pronounced arches when their feet are held up and relaxed. The arches disappear under weight because the feet roll too far inward. This is the most common foot defect and can cause a number of injuries, including knee problems, arch pain, shinsplints, and Achilles tendonitis. Some people with excessive pronation will require

---

*Pronation is the normal action of the foot that cushions its landing. The foot rolls onto the ground, with the outside of the heel striking first and the ball and inside of the foot progressively taking weight. At the same time, the angle between the foot and the lower leg is decreasing and the leg is rotating inward on the hip joint. This action also allows the foot to adapt to varying terrain. The opposite action—supination—occurs as your weight passes over the foot. The foot then becomes a rigid lever and allows you to take off. Excessive pronation occurs when the foot rolls over too fast and doesn't start rotating back soon enough. This puts extra stress on muscles and tendons and transmits rotational forces up into the knee and hip.

custom-made foot supports called orthotics made by a podiatrist (foot specialist) to run without injury, but most will be able to get adequate support from well-designed shoes. Good ones to try are those made by Etonic, which have a special support designed by runner-podiatrist Rob Roy McGregor. Good support is a function of the whole construction of the shoe, not just the arch area. If a thick sole is used for cushioning, some flare in the sole is generally required to keep the shoes from acting like stilts, but the amount of flare desirable depends on the shoe and the runner. A wide flare helps to stabilize many runners' feet if the rest of the shoe is firm, too; but other runners develop ankle pain if they wear shoes with flared heels, because the shoes flatten their feet against the ground too rapidly.

Solid construction of the shoe's upper is important, though naturally this should be managed with as little added weight as possible. A skimpy upper will soon start to cave in and won't provide proper foot support. The heel counter in particular should hold the heel of the foot firmly.

Shoe maintenance is as important as choosing a good pair in the first place. Significant wear on one edge of the sole, especially at the heel, can completely change the way your foot lands. Differences of as little as an eighth-inch can result in injuries if they are allowed to persist. Those people who are most affected by these changes—the ones with abnormal feet—are just the ones who tend to wear shoes off quickly at one edge. Replacing either soles or shoes is a costly business, so the most sensible alternative is to keep the soles built up so that they never wear unevenly. The best way to do this is with a hot glue gun, an electrically heated device that melts glue sticks and dispenses the hot glue through a nozzle. The guns and glue sticks can be purchased in a hardware store. Use the glue to keep building up those areas of the sole that tend to wear down, applying a thin layer whenever necessary to keep the sole even all the way across. Proper use of the glue gun will maintain the original pair of soles until the uppers fall apart.

STRUCTURAL DEFECTS
OF THE FEET AND LEGS

Most running injuries can be traced back to training errors, muscle imbalances, failure to stretch regularly, or poor shoes. Runners (and sometimes doctors and podiatrists, too) often tend to look for exotic causes when the real source of difficulty is both common and obvious. But many runners *do* have weaknesses in their feet or legs, and these can cause intractable overuse injuries. If you can look back at your training record and be sure that you haven't been pushing too hard, structural problems are the most likely cause of your trouble. Try to analyze your gait, and see a podiatrist or an orthopedic specialist. (Injuries can be discussed only briefly here; they are covered in far more detail in my *Running Without Pain: A Guide to the Prevention and Treatment of Running Injuries,* Dial Press, 1980.) Discuss the problem thoroughly with any specialist you see to make sure that the analysis makes sense to you. A good trainer or a doctor knowledgeable in running injuries will know more about injuries and treatment than you ever could, but you get more information from the way you feel while you are running than an outsider can accumulate even with the most thorough examination. You should insist on being a full partner in your own treatment.

The most common structural problem is excessive pronation, which has already been mentioned. Besides feet that appear flat when weighted, there are some other obvious signs. People who pronate excessively tend to wear down the soles of their shoes on the far outside of the heel and the far inside of the toe. Normal feet wear the soles just slightly to the outside of the center of the heel and fairly evenly on the inside half of the sole in front of the ball of the foot. The wear occurs mainly during takeoff and landing, so the points of wear show where your foot lands and how you push off. Pushing off well to the inside edge of the shoe means that the toes are not sharing the load of takeoff. The foot rolls too far in when it strikes, and it doesn't move far enough back to become a rigid lever for take-

off. Another common foot defect that causes excessive pronation is Morton's foot, which can usually be recognized by a big
toe that is quite a bit shorter than the second toe.

Some injuries that are common among those who pronate
excessively are pain in the Achilles tendons; strains in the plantar fascia (the bands that stretch like bowstrings across the arch
of the foot); pain or bumps on the bottoms of the heels where
the plantar fascia attach; shinsplints; and pain on the inside of
the knee or behind the kneecap, especially when you're des-
cending stairs or after you've been sitting for a long time.

Shoes that provide better support or inserted arch supports
will often help runners with feet that pronate excessively. If
these remedies don't bring about a quick improvement, however, you should see a podiatrist or orthopedist who can build
orthotics to provide better support for your feet. Try to see a
specialist who has a good reputation among other runners.

A less common defect in the feet is excessive rigidity—the
feet don't pronate enough to absorb the shock of impact. People with very high arches often have overly rigid feet. Another
sign to watch for is a pattern of wear along the outside half of
the sole from heel to toe. Tendon and knee problems, especially on the outside of the knee, are also common among runners whose feet are too rigid. Shoes with better cushioning may
help; but I suggest that if you seem to have this difficulty and
sustain overuse injuries, you see a podiatrist. Rigid feet are less
common than excessive pronation, but they are more difficult
to treat. Orthotics often help.

Bow legs and knock knees are easier to detect and can cause
a number of overuse injuries. If you have a hard time touching
your knees together when standing straight with your feet
touching, you have bow legs. Injuries often occur that are similar to those caused by excessive pronation. If you have difficulty touching your feet together while standing straight with
your knees together, you have knock knees. Injuries to the outside of the knees, ankles, and hips are common.

Unequal leg length can cause many difficulties, but it is much
harder to detect than one might think. If you have any

frequent injury problems and your shoulders and hips seem to tilt a little in opposite directions when you are standing relaxed, this may be the cause. Even specialists have a hard time analyzing this problem. The only happy note is that treatment is simple—inserting a heel lift in the shoe of the short leg for temporary correction, and increasing the height of the wedges in the heels of the running shoe for a long-term solution.

Other structural irregularities in the feet and legs can be either subtler or more obvious. Because runners subject their legs to so much stress, even trivial irregularities can cause problems. It stands to reason that those with obvious misalignments in their feet should see a good podiatrist if they experience any overuse injuries. Subtler problems cannot even be summarized here. The feet (or one foot) can be angled in one direction in the heel and in another across the toes, while also being oriented askew from the hip or knee. Problems in the lower back can radiate down to the legs. A good orthopedist or podiatrist who is sympathetic to runners and understands the mechanics of the sport can work wonders in curing overuse injuries. Don't let your symptoms drag on and become chronic before seeking help. By the same token, however, don't accept anyone's diagnosis without question if it doesn't make sense to you. As in all fields, there are hack podiatrists and orthopedists along with brilliant diagnosticians.

TREATMENT AND FIRST AID

The standard initial treatment for all running injuries, besides rest, is I.C.E.—icing, compression, and elevation. This is particularly important with sudden pain as well as with muscle pulls. Ice in a towel or an ice pack, rubbed on the painful area twenty minutes of every hour, will reduce circulation to the injured area and directly alleviate the pain. Since most running injuries involve tissue damage, there is often internal damage accompanied by bleeding, which then causes swelling. The swelling in turn postpones healing and prolongs pain. Icing, compression with an elastic bandage, and elevation of the injured part reduce the bleeding and swelling, so that pain is reduced and later healing is promoted.

Muscle tears are the easiest injuries to diagnose. A sudden sharp pain in the body of the muscle will usually halt you in your tracks. Unless there is a deformity indicating a complete rupture, diagnosis of seriousness has to wait until twenty-four hours after the injury, with I.C.E. proceeding immediately. If you limp only a little the next day, you can treat yourself. If you can't put significant stress on the muscle, see a good trainer or doctor. Treatment for any muscle tear, small or large, is rest, followed by careful stretching and mild strengthening exercises during recovery. The stretching prevents the muscle from shortening during healing as scar tissue forms. Exercises contribute to proper healing and prevent reinjury. Muscle pulls take from two to six weeks to heal.

Tendon pain should be treated very seriously. Achilles tendon injuries are common in distance runners, and they are often made worse when people try to run through them. If bouncing on your toes causes sharp pain (or if you can't even get up onto your toes), you probably have torn the tendon. Pinching along its length may locate a spot that is painful to squeeze. If so, there is definitely a tear at this point. Torn tendons require a complete layoff for a period of two to six weeks, combined with careful stretching once the tendon begins to heal. Tendons have a very poor blood supply and heal slowly. You should see a physician in cases of torn tendons. Injections of cortisone, which have frequently been used to treat tendonitis, should never be used if this is the diagnosis—they weaken the tendon further and mask pain, so it's easy to injure the tendon even more. A single shot can sometimes be useful to treat inflammations in the same area, like bursitis or inflammation of the tendon sheath. Generalized pain around the area of a tendon that cannot be localized to one spot may be an inflammation of the sheath (tenosynovitis) or irritation and inflammation of a fluid-filled sac or bursa that cushions a spot where a tendon rubs over bone (bursitis). In the heel area, bursitis hurts rather like a damaged tendon, but is not significantly worse when you bounce on your toes and cannot be localized to one point on the tendon.

A sharp or boring pain at a spot along the path of a bone, especially if it is sensitive to pressure at that spot, usually indicates a stress fracture of the bone. Hairline cracks form after repeated overstress or a sudden force. When this occurs, weight must be taken off the bone for several weeks. Stress fractures can sometimes be diagnosed only by manual pressure against the bone, but they will show up on an X ray after they have begun to heal. Structural defects or overtraining are the most frequent causes of stress fractures. They are most common in the shinbone, the anklebones, and the metatarsals—the bones leading out toward the toes along the top of the foot.

Sharp, shooting pains that radiate from one point to another indicate some involvement of the nerves. A nerve itself may be inflamed, or it may be transmitting pain from one injured area along the path of the nerve. Structural problems or overtraining may cause such problems; but nerves can also become inflamed for reasons that are not completely understood, particularly when the athlete overtrains. See a physician if such problems persist.

Knee problems can result from overtraining, from shoes that don't provide enough cushioning, from old injuries, or from defects in the feet or legs. Try well-cushioned shoes that provide good support, together with reduced training. If problems persist, see an orthopedist or a podiatrist. Those who pronate excessively are likely to have knee difficulties unless they can provide support for the inside of the foot. If home remedies don't work quickly, see a podiatrist. If you have old injuries, running may cause flare-ups. *Don't try to run through pain.* You may have to build up very slowly. If reduced training doesn't work, see an orthopedist, preferably one sympathetic to running. Persisting in training despite knee pain is likely to cause permanent damage.

CHAPTER XV

RACING AND OTHER CHALLENGES

SOME OF THE attractions of racing and its advantages for the dedicated runner have been mentioned in earlier chapters. Racing provides you with a chance to put years of training together in a sustained effort to see how well you can do. It is a physical and psychological challenge that can also be a pleasant social occasion. Races can be fun or they can be grueling efforts, depending on the length, the conditions, and your attitude. Unless you run races as training runs, however, they have a quite different flavor and effect on your body than your day-to-day running has. Racing by its very nature stimulates maximum effort, to push you harder than you would go in your regular running. The same is true of special challenges you may choose for their particular appeal to you, like exceptional point-to-point runs and mountain runs. If you pick them as a focus for your training, they take on a special aura that enables you to summon a far-greater-than-average effort from your body.

I think that it is a mistake to view racing in the same casual light as you view training runs. But by this I don't mean that you have to take racing very seriously, as though it were on a par with more serious challenges in life. Running for most of us is a recreational activity, and it should be fun. Considering races as you would training runs, however, robs them of their unique quality. Races should involve more effort than training runs—that's what they are for. Even races run in preparation for more important competitions later on are still quite different from day-to-day running. Quite a few club racers disagree with this point of view. They like to race once or twice every week, never too hard, and these runs are like fast training runs in many ways. They may take some races more seriously than others, or they may run all of their races in this spirit. The dangers of running races frequently at top effort have already been pointed out. If you simply like to run races regularly at a good effort, by all means go ahead. Personally, I would rather take my recreational and training runs on quiet roads and trails, saving the racing atmosphere for its own special stimulus.

RACING FUNDAMENTALS

Racing distances range from sprints of sixty yards or so to hundred-mile races; from twenty-four-hour runs during which each competitor covers the maximum possible distance to multi-day events over some exceptional route or distance. The differences in the demands of such a variety of races are enormous, and the training and tactics involved are similarly divergent. Most of the discussion here will be of road racing, because this is where the incredible growth of the last few years has occurred. Road racing was the ugly duckling of competitive running until quite recently, arousing little interest and getting almost no help from the official governing organizations of amateur athletics. The situation is reversed now, because of the tremendous interest generated by road racing among both runners and spectators. In most parts of the country it is now easy to find well-organized road races of almost any distance, from two or three miles to the marathon. The revival has been due almost completely to the efforts of road racers themselves. Local groups of runners have organized their own races to provide the competition they want and have learned to handle the mechanics so well that most of these races are extremely well organized.

Road racing has major advantages for most runners, because of both availability and mechanics. Few track races are open to runners who are not competing for schools or already running at quite a high level. Those who are interested in the shorter events that are best run on the track can organize such competition, of course, if a local school track can be reserved for the occasion. Some clubs around the country do put on such events for citizen racers. Track events cannot handle the level of competition that has become normal in road races, however. It is now commonplace for a thousand runners to participate in a road race. There are dozens of races that attract several thousand participants each. A properly managed road race can accommodate these numbers together with a wide range of ability ranging from joggers to world-class competitors. Everyone can have a good time and run at his or her own level of competition. It would be impossible to run track races on this scale.

Advance registration is required in many road races to simplify administration and make things go more smoothly for everyone. When numbers are issued and names recorded, the chaos that can develop before a race is greatly reduced and the organizers are permitted to prepare properly for the number of people who will actually be running. One good alternative for low-key local races is to dispense with numbers altogether. Under this scheme the timer calls out your elapsed time as you cross the finish line, and you give your time and name to the recorder. In more formal races, however, getting your race packet in advance makes everything simpler both for you and for the race officials.

Racers in large events may be seeded by the organizers or may be expected to sort themselves out. The accepted etiquette in races with starts that have limited width and a large field of runners is to place yourself in the pack behind the starting line approximately in the position you would expect to finish. If you are planning to run only 7½-minute miles, don't squeeze into the front of the starting field so that many faster runners will be forced to get past you early in the race. The tendency to start too fast is always a problem in races, anyway, and you will only make proper pacing harder by moving up with the elite racers.

If you are aiming at a race as a goal for months of training, you should choose it carefully, making sure it is compatible with your own objectives. A race that has a reputation for being well managed will be less likely to result in frustration, particularly for the beginner, than one with a poorly marked course, incorrectly called splits (times at intermediate points along the course), and aid stations with inadequate supplies of drinks. Similarly, if you are interested in running a personal best time, you should try to pick a race that is likely to offer good conditions for this kind of effort. Hot weather and hilly courses don't make for fast times. A high-altitude marathon is not the one to choose if you are trying to run under three hours for the first time.

POINTING TOWARD A RACE

During your last couple of weeks of sharpening, you should be pointing toward the races in which you most want to do well. If you plan to run on the track or in short road races, you should continue to include interval training sessions after your initial six weeks of sharpening, reducing the work load and emphasizing short, sharp work on leg speed. For longer events, you need to concentrate more on time trials over distances shorter than the event in which you want to race and pace work to learn the exact cadence you want to use during the race.

The longer the race, the more important it is to develop an exact sense of pace. If you want to run a 10-mile road race in 55 minutes, you need to learn exactly how it feels to do 5½-minute miles. The best way to do this is to insert pace work regularly into your workouts—not to push yourself hard, but to concentrate on the feeling and rhythm of that pace. Run a measured section in a long training run one-half to one mile long at exactly the right pace, concentrating on how your breathing feels and how your legs and arms move at this pace. During the early minutes of the race, concentrate on settling into this rhythm, ignoring the excitement and chaos around you until you have found your pace. At the first split, check your pace and adjust it if necessary.

Training for the conditions of a particular race or run can be critical both physically and psychologically. A very hilly course is not only demanding to the muscles and the cardiopulmonary system; it is very intimidating unless you have been training enough on the hills to be confident of your ability to handle them.

TRAINING FOR HOT WEATHER

One of the most important factors in training for particular races is temperature. This can be a particular problem if you are pointing toward a spring race that may have hot, humid conditions and are training in a climate and season that are cool and dry. The Boston Marathon, for example, can present ideal running conditions for a fast, comfortable race—or it can be very hot and humid. If you have not acclimatized to hot-weather running recently, hot conditions in a long race can be devastating. I first ran Boston in very hot conditions after training through the Colorado winter and early spring. I was massacred; I lost a full minute per mile by the end of the race and walked stiffly for days. I was considerably better off than many others, however, since about a third of the finishers required medical attention. That race taught me my lesson about acclimatizing to heat before racing in it.

Runners vary a good deal in their ability to run in the heat. Frank Shorter, for example, is known for his heat tolerance. He keeps a normal fast pace long after other world-class marathoners wilt. Bill Rodgers, on the other hand, surely the best U.S. marathoner at the time this is being written, is not very heat tolerant, despite the fact that he lives and trains in the Boston area, which has hot, muggy summers. He dropped out of both the 1976 and 1977 Boston races because of the heat, but he has won the race in three other years, setting both a course and a U.S. record in it.

Regardless of your basic heat tolerance, however, proper acclimatization will enable you to compete credibly, judge your ability accurately in heat, and beat a lot of racers in a hot competition who would normally trounce you. Most racers just don't take the trouble to acclimatize, particularly for the early hot races. The acclimatized runner can process liquid more quickly and pump it out to cool the skin. When you have been running regularly in the heat, the circulation to your skin improves, enabling you to dissipate heat faster. You lose fewer electrolytes in sweat, so your body chemistry does not become imbalanced and inefficient even after large losses of sweat.

Acclimatization is straightforward. All you have to do is to run in the heat. Running in the cool of the day is more pleasant and easier on your body, but it won't prepare you for hot-weather running. Run three times a week in the heat of the day for a month. If it isn't hot enough out, wear a sweatsuit. If this is comfortable, wear more sweats. You have to be uncomfortably hot to acclimatize. But *do not try to go without liquids.* It won't help you to acclimatize, and it abuses your body dangerously. I usually leave jugs of water along my long training routes during hot-weather training.

Clothing can help in both hot- and cool-weather races if you are a little better prepared than others. Light-colored clothes reflect heat better. A light, porous jersey will often keep you cooler than running with no shirt at all. A light, well-ventilated cap that will reflect the sun and can be doused with water or filled with ice is often a real help in staying cool during hot races. When the weather seems changeable, with the possibility of a cold headwind coming up, I like to carry a spare piece of clothing around my waist for a long race. A cold headwind coming up in a marathon when you are running in shorts and singlet can stiffen your muscles and slow you down in the last part of the race. A lightweight nylon shell that you can put on while you are running can make the difference.

An important final note on running in the heat, particularly when conditions are also humid: Be careful. A runner moving at a good pace generates tremendous amounts of waste heat as a by-product of muscular action—enough to ensure that you'll stay warm with little clothing in rather cold weather. This waste heat must be dissipated to the environment or the temperature of the body will begin to rise. Humans cannot stand a very significant rise in the overall temperature of the body; an increase of a few degrees will disrupt the functioning of the body, and a few more degrees will result first in brain damage and then in death. Don't try to heat-acclimatize until you are already in good shape. If you feel weak or dizzy in either a training run or a race, slow down to a walk and find some shade to lie down in. If you see anyone weaving in a race, get them off the course. Heat exhaustion, the symptoms of which are dizziness, fatigue, and sometimes pale skin, is the result of the cooling system going awry and blood pressure falling. Sit down before you fall down. More dangerous heat stroke is less common among runners; the primary symptom is very hot, flushed, dry skin. Immediate cooling with whatever means are available is essential to prevent death. The victim should be rushed to a hospital.

A runner who has trained adequately in the heat will have a far better feeling for what is happening during a hot-weather race than the unacclimatized runner. The best strategy in such races is to start at a slower pace than you otherwise would and to do everything you can to stay cool: drinking, dousing yourself with water, putting ice in your cap. Run within your limits. Most of the people who start out fast in a hot-weather race will fade and come back to you. The longer the race, the truer this will be. Humidity has an additive effect with heat. Much of your body's cooling comes from the heat that can be lost by evaporating sweat from the skin. The higher the humidity, the less rapidly sweat will evaporate, and the less cooling effect it has. This is why you seem to sweat so much more in humid conditions. Much of the perspiration just pours off your body without evaporating. Cold drinks and cold water poured over your skin are particularly helpful in these conditions. Remember, too, that heavier people are more vulnerable to heat. They have less surface area for cooling per pound of body weight.

DRINKING DURING A RACE

Cool drinks are a major help in a long, hot race. They provide direct cooling first and then allow the body to replenish the liquid supplies that are lost in perspiration, permitting further cooling. They are also important in maintaining efficient muscle operation. The acclimatized runner loses most moisture from the tissues rather than from the blood, so large amounts of water can be lost without danger of heat injury. The chemical balance of the cells can be upset by the loss of liquid, however, and the muscles lose in efficiency. Liquid losses are a major factor in limiting the runner's capacity during the later stages of a long race, particularly in hot, humid conditions. Most runners should drink often in races of longer than ten kilometers or six miles.

Drinking just before the race is a help. If you drink too long before, you will simply lose the liquid as urine, but drinking a few minutes before the race will allow you to start absorbing liquid during the first few miles. The early aid stations in a race are the important ones to make; you'll be thirstier later on, but you won't be able to absorb the liquid until after the race is over. Large quantities of liquid will bloat you, but a cup every five miles or so keeps you from dehydrating so badly. Drink more often in a very hot race. There is no point except comfort in drinking during the last four or five miles of a race unless you have slowed to below eight-minute miles.

Electrolyte-replacement drinks are nice after a race. Whether they do any particular good during a race is open to question. There are also major disagreements among experts as to how much glucose or other sugar can be absorbed during a race. If one can absorb it, glucose during a long race like a marathon is helpful, since it provides some replacement blood sugar and postpones the exhaustion of reserves. Some authorities believe that fairly high concentrations of glucose or table sugar can be absorbed rather rapidly. Others have found that sweet drinks retard the emptying of the stomach, so that liquid cannot be absorbed so rapidly, increasing dehydration and heat buildup. Personally, I feel that excessively sweet drinks do interfere with liquid absorption and I recommend that electrolyte-replacement drinks or orange juice be diluted half-and-half with water. You can do this during a race by alternating electrolyte drinks with water at the aid stations.

One thing that the experts agree on is that you shouldn't take sweet drinks much before the race. At this stage, the sugar will cause the insulin level in the blood to rise, negating the possible beneficial effect of the beverage. If you are taking a drink with a sweetener in it for energy, drink it just a few minutes before the race. Once you are exercising hard, the insulin reaction won't occur, and you will get some benefit from the drink. There is also no point in taking any sweets for races of less than twenty minutes' or a half-hour's duration, since blood sugar won't be used much for fuel until then.

GENERAL RACING TACTICS

Remember that the most efficient way to run a race is normally at an even pace. This is why learning pacing can be so important for running your best time. If you start too slowly, you won't be able to make up the time later on. If you start too fast (and most people do), you will fade badly toward the end. Most people who think they run at an even pace actually slow badly at the end. Other tactics are important only against runners who are more or less at your own level.

It stands to reason, then, that in a race where you are not in serious competition for the lead or against someone else (another person in your class or a friendly rival, perhaps), your best race tactic will be to run an even pace. Ignore the other runners until you have homed in on your pace—then pick some other people running at the same speed to run with. Chances are that if you use this strategy well, you will have lots of people to pass at the end, giving you a good psychological lift. Be particularly wary of going out fast in the heat or in severe hills. I have done well in some mountain races by starting slowly at the back of the pack and watching the competition drop off as the climbing begins.

In races where you are either competing to win or to beat a particular known group, tactics become important. There are endless variations, but most of them boil down to attempting to force your competition to run *your* race. This is crucial psychologically, because you feel comfortable, while the other person is apprehensive. Thus, the strategy of the runner who takes an early lead and holds it is to set the pace, making others feel that you are so strong you can't be caught. Often this is merely a psychological game. You look strong as you lead up the hill even though you are as tired as everyone else. It is a dangerous strategy, though, unless you are really strong. The person behind can often save work by tucking in behind and using a leader for a windscreen, making a move at a propitious moment.

Similar tactics abound, depending on the strengths and reputations of those who use them. If you have a poor kick at the end and your opponent has an excellent one, you want to build up your distance long before the finish. High-altitude runners at a high-altitude race will try to force the pace early to capitalize on their conditioning, while runners from a lower elevation in the same race will try to hold the pace down and use their speed at the end.

Remember, though, that all good tactics have to be based on a good understanding of your own capacity. If you know the pace you can hold, don't go out with the leaders at a much faster rate: you'll only crash and burn. If you hold steady at your best pace, either you'll find that others come back within your reach later in the race or you'll at least make your best possible showing. Usually it is better to save the fancier strategies until you have acquired more racing experience. Even then, you will find that a good sense of pacing will often allow you to win against many opponents who have a lot more basic speed.

CONCLUSION

For the serious runner, the positive side of the sport does not require endless praise; the sense of physical well-being, mental relaxation, and diversion from the stresses of everyday life are familiar experiences. Running can also provide a series of pleasant challenges, refreshingly different from those that we experience elsewhere in our lives, providing that we retain the sense of recreation that should be at the center of the sport. Running is recreation in both the usual sense of the word—a diversion that allows relaxation from the more serious side of life—and in the original meaning—a re-creation of the self at a more profound level.

Most of the time, however, running should be fun. It is not likely to provide profound philosophical experiences very often, any more than other facets of life will. The challenges also have to be kept in perspective if they are not to become obsessions. With a proper balance running can make our lives richer and provide a series of satisfactions that will last for decades.

ADDITIONAL READING

THOUGH THERE IS a wealth of literature about track and field, the information available on distance running is far scantier, especially as regards those questions that are most important to the dedicated older runner. Serious long-distance runners of all ages have been training and competing for many years, but they were usually ignored. Those who got hurt either managed to cure themselves or quit; training methods for this kind of running were considered only by a few pioneers like Arthur Lydiard and Ernst van Aaken. The available material can be expected to increase enormously in the next few years, but the runner still has to search through a lot of chaff in order to find a few grains of wheat.

PERIODICALS. Probably the best of the current crop of running magazines is *The Runner:* $12 per year, from P.O. Box 2730, Boulder, CO 80321. The long-time standard publication for distance runners has been *Runner's World:* $13 per year, from 1400 Stierlin Rd., Mountain View, CA 94043. *Running Times* is another magazine aimed at the serious distance runner and publishes separate editions for the East and West to allow printing more complete race schedules: $12 per year, from 12808 Occoquan Rd., Woodbridge, VA 22192. *Marathoner* is a quarterly spin-off publication from *Runner's World:* $10 per year from Box 366, Mountain View, CA 94043. The standard publication of running results in the U.S., still mostly oriented toward the track as the name indicates, is *Track & Field News:* $12 per year, from Box 296, Los Altos, CA 94022.

GENERAL. Two basic books on distance running are the author's *The Runner's Book* (New York: Scribner's, 1978) and *The Runner's Handbook* by Bob Glover and Jack Shepherd (New York: Penguin, 1978). Books written by notable runners are among the most informative sources of information. Some good ones are Roger Bannister's *The Four Minute Mile* (New York: Dodd, Mead, 1955); *The Self-Made Olympian* by Ron Dawes (Mountain View, CA: World, 1977); Jack Foster's *Tale of the Ancient Marathoner* (Mountain View, CA: World, 1974); *The Serious Runner's Handbook* by Tom Osler (Mountain View, CA: World, 1978); and *On the Run* by Marty Liquori and Skip Myslenski (New York: Morrow, 1979).

The views of the most influential modern coaches can be found in *Running the Lydiard Way* by Arthur Lydiard and Garth Gilmour (1978), the *Van Aaken Method* by Ernst van Aaken (1976), and *Training with Cerutty* by Larry Myers (1977) (all Mountain View, CA: World).

PHYSIOLOGY. The two best texts on the physiology of exercise are H. A. De Vries's *Physiology of Exercise for Physical Education and Athletics* (Dubuque, IA: Wm. C. Brown, 1966) and *Textbook of Work Physiology* by Per-Olaf Astrand and Kaare Rodahl (New York: McGraw-Hill, 1970). Specifics on the physiology of running can be found in David Costill's *What Research Tells the Coach About Distance Running* (Washington, DC: American Alliance for Health, Physical Education, and Recreation, 1968) and *A Scientific Approach to Distance Running* (Los Altos, CA: *Track & Field News,* 1979); *Conditioning for Distance Running* by Jack Daniels, Robert Fitts, and George Sheehan (New York: Wiley, 1978); and in *The Long Distance Runner,* edited by Paul Milvy (New York: Urizen, 1978).

TRAINING METHODS. Collections of information on the methods used by different runners provide a useful perspective on details of training. The best is Fred Wilt's *How They Train* (Los Altos, CA: *Track & Field News,* 1959 and later editions). Joe Henderson's *Road Racers and Their Training* (Los Altos, CA: *Track & Field News,* 1970) has an interesting selection, old enough so that we know what happened to the runners during the subsequent decade. Tom Ecker, Fred Wilt, and Jim Hay have compiled several guides analyzing and illustrating the technique and style of champions in both running and field events. A good one is *Olympic Track and Field Techniques* (West Nyack, NY: Park, 1974).

EXERCISES. The best book on resistance training for runners is John Jesse's *Strength, Power and Muscular Endurance for Runners and Hurdlers* (Pasadena, CA: Athletic Press, 1971). For stretching techniques, the discipline of yoga is the most thorough flexibility program; B.K.S. Iyengar's *Light on Yoga* (New York: Schocken, 1966) will keep anyone busy for years. A more relaxed but still fairly thorough treatment can be found in *Stretching* by Bob Anderson (P.O. Box 2734, Fullerton, CA: privately published, 1975).

MEDICAL. Injuries and ways to avoid them are discussed in detail in the author's *Running Without Pain: A Guide to the Prevention and Treatment of Running Injuries* (New York: Dial Press, 1980). Also useful are *Dr. George Sheehan's Medical Advice for Runners* (Mountain View, CA: World, 1978); *The Foot Book* by Harry F. Hlavac (Mountain View, CA: World, 1977); and *The Sports-medicine Book* by Gabe Mirkin and Marshall Hoffman (Boston: Little, Brown, 1978).

INDEX